The Texas
Polygamist
Raid

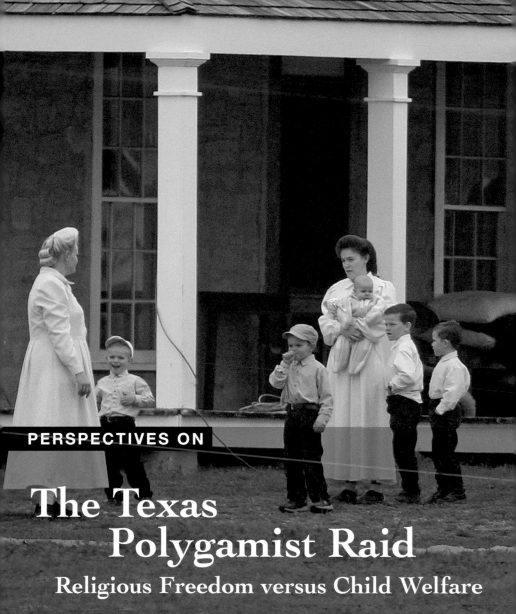

PERSPECTIVES ON

The Texas Polygamist Raid

Religious Freedom versus Child Welfare

KATIE MARSICO

Marshall Cavendish
Benchmark
New York

Other Marshall Cavendish Offices: Marshall Cavendish International (Asia) Private Limited, 1 New Industrial Road, Singapore 536196 • Marshall Cavendish International (Thailand) Co Ltd. 253 Asoke, 12th Flr, Sukhumvit 21 Road, Klongtoey Nua, Wattana, Bangkok 10110, Thailand • Marshall Cavendish (Malaysia) Sdn Bhd, Times Subang, Lot 46, Subang Hi-Tech Industrial Park, Batu Tiga, 40000 Shah Alam, Selangor Darul Ehsan, Malaysia

Marshall Cavendish is a trademark of Times Publishing Limited

All websites were available and accurate when this book was sent to press.

Library of Congress Cataloging-in-Publication Data

Marsico, Katie, 1980–
The Texas polygamist raid : religious freedom versus child welfare / by Katie Marsico.
p. cm. — (Perspectives on)
Includes bibliographical references and index.
Summary: "Provides comprehensive information on the Texas polygamist raid and the differing perspectives accompanying it"—Provided by publisher.
ISBN 978-1-60870-449-1 (print) ISBN 978-1-60870-721-8 (ebook)
1. Child welfare—Texas—Juvenile literature. 2. Polygamy—Texas—Juvenile literature. 3. Fundamentalist Church of Jesus Christ of Latter-Day Saints—Juvenile literature. I. Title.
HV742.T4M37 2011
364.15'55409764876—dc22
2010016038

Expert Reader: Jan Shipps, Professor Emerita, History and Religious Studies, Indiana University–Perdue University, Indianapolis

Editor: Christine Florie
Publisher: Michelle Bisson
Art Director: Anahid Hamparian
Series Designer: Sonia Chaghatzbanian

Photo research by Marybeth Kavanagh

Cover photo by *AP Photo/Eric Gay*

The photographs in this book are used by permission and through the courtesy of: *Getty Images*: Mike Terry/Deseret Morning News, 2-3, 19, 52; Stephan Gladieu, 16; George Frey, 59; August Miller/Deseret Morning News, 76, 84; *Newscom.com*: Trent Nelson/Salt Lake Tribune/Rapport Press, 8; *AP Photo*: Tony Gutierrez, 11, 22, 49; Douglas C. Pizac, 23; Eric Gay, 33; Susan Walsh, 44; LM Otero, 67; Harry Cabluck, 79; *Reuters*: Jessica Rinaldi, 40

Printed in Malaysia (T)
1 3 5 6 4 2

Contents

Introduction

THE FUNDAMENTALIST CHURCH of Jesus Christ of Latter-Day Saints (FLDS) was formed in the 1930s and, by 2008, was no stranger to intrigue and scandal. Women clad in nineteenth-century prairie garb and men who took multiple wives raised Americans' eyebrows and stirred the interest of authorities, who regarded polygamy as an illegal practice. At the same time, however, the U.S. Constitution guaranteed citizens' rights to religious freedom, no matter how unorthodox a faith they chose to follow.

Yet as of early 2008 child-welfare officials had come to suspect that events at the Yearning for Zion (YFZ) Ranch just outside Eldorado, Texas, were more than slightly irregular. In fact, when they and law-enforcement agents made their way onto the 1,700-acre FLDS property on April 3, 2008, they did so because they believed children were at risk of abuse. Acting on a disturbing series of phone calls to a domestic-violence hotline the previous month, they scoured the ranch in search of evidence of sexual misconduct.

When they reportedly observed several teenage mothers and heard accounts of men coercing underage brides into polygamous marriages, they began removing children from their homes. In the process 439 minors were taken from their parents and placed in temporary state custody. The highly emotional controversy that followed pitted Americans' longing to protect their religious liberties against their desire to safeguard child welfare.

From Child Protective Services officials who insisted they were only trying to prevent sexual abuse to FLDS members who declared that they were being unjustly persecuted, key players voiced their perspectives on the raid. While their vantage points frequently clashed, those involved in the raid forced U.S. citizens to consider which was a higher priority: the safety of children or religious freedom. Just as important, events at the YFZ Ranch in April 2008 prompted Americans to contemplate if there was any way to support one issue without jeopardizing the other.

One

Faith amid Fears of Abuse

IN EARLY APRIL 2008 chaos erupted at the Yearning for Zion (YFZ) Ranch just outside the town of Eldorado in Schleicher County, Texas. On April 3 of that year, law-enforcement officials and child-welfare authorities descended on the 1,700-acre compound, which was home to more than seven hundred members of the Fundamentalist Church of Jesus Christ of Latter-Day Saints (FLDS). Since the FLDS had purchased the property in 2003, outsiders had speculated about the particular beliefs and activities of the people who lived there. Residents considered themselves "Original Mormons" or "Fundamentalist Mormons." It was a particular aspect of their faith that had begun to arouse suspicion.

It appeared that some FLDS members were engaged in polygamy, or plural marriage—a practice that is considered a felony in the United States but that is regarded by certain religions as the pathway to salvation. In the past, officials frequently had turned a blind eye toward suspected offenders. The exception to this rule occurred when child welfare was at stake, with grown men taking child brides or forcing underage girls into marital unions against their will. In the spring

Following allegations of sexual abuse of minors, Texas authorities took custody of more than four hundred children at the YFZ Ranch.

of 2008, Texas authorities felt they had reason to believe such circumstances existed at the mysterious YFZ Ranch.

In late March of that year, workers at a domestic-violence hotline were contacted by a caller who described herself as a pregnant sixteen-year-old girl named Sarah Barlow. She claimed to live on the ranch and explained to the social-service employees that she was a victim of both sexual and physical abuse. Responding to Sarah's cry for help, Texas Rangers and Child Protective Services (CPS) headed to the YFZ compound with a warrant to search the premises on April 3, 2008.

While they met with no armed resistance, tensions on the ranch heightened in the days that followed, as one grandmother who asked to be identified only as Nancy later recalled. She told reporters with the *Deseret News* that Rangers and CPS workers entered her home and began separating and interrogating all the children who were present. According to Nancy, confusion and panic reigned as it became apparent that authorities intended to take the youngsters into their custody.

"[They] didn't give us an explanation of what they were doing," she said. "They told us, 'We're going to take the children unless you tell us who are their mothers.' But we still weren't saying anything." After she and her relatives continued to maintain their silence in the face of what they perceived as a terrifying and unprovoked intrusion, law-enforcement officials started calling for backup.

Nancy, who was holding an infant when authorities made their way into her house, tearfully relayed to journalists how one officer "poked [his] face into [my] face" and ordered her to "give me that baby!" Though she refused at first, Nancy

Law-enforcement officials assist residents of the YFZ Ranch as they prepare to leave their homes in April 2008.

eventually was forced to stand by and watch helplessly as police took several of her children and grandchildren into their custody and ushered them onto buses. They were among the 439 minors who were removed from the ranch during the first few weeks of April 2008.

CPS officials insisted that their actions were based on evidence that the children in question "had been abused or

From LDS to FLDS: Changing Perspectives on Plural Marriage

Though the FLDS was established in the 1930s, the Church of Jesus Christ of Latter-Day Saints (LDS) dates back an additional hundred years. Founded by Joseph Smith in 1830, the church initially supported plural marriage. It wasn't long, however, before this practice came under scrutiny by the U.S. government.

For starters, Congress passed the Morrill Anti-Bigamy Act in July 1862. This legislation banned polygamy and limited the landholdings any religious group could claim in a U.S. territory. Since the church owned a substantial amount of property in Utah Territory—which encompassed portions of present-day Nevada, Utah, Colorado, and Wyoming—the act had the potential to limit both the growth of the LDS and the freedom of its members to practice plural marriage.

Yet many Mormons chose to ignore the federal legislation, arguing that their right to engage in polygamy was protected under the First Amendment. By the 1870s, though, their sense of security was shaken. In 1878 the U.S. Supreme Court handed down a famous ruling in a court case known as *Reynolds* v. *the United States*. An LDS member named George Reynolds had been convicted of bigamy based on the Morrill Anti-Bigamy Act. When the case was ultimately presented to the Supreme Court, judges stated that a person's devotion to what he or she considers a religious duty is not a sufficient defense against criminal charges.

By 1890 the LDS officially denounced polygamy, though it took a few more decades for the majority of church members to completely turn their back on the practice. In the meantime, several new forms of Mormonism, including the FLDS, emerged. Many of these congregations continue to embrace plural marriage, despite the fact that this element of their faith has prompted ongoing clashes with the U.S. government.

were at immediate risk of future abuse." To back up their allegations, they pointed to everything from pregnant teenagers to beds found in the YFZ temple that they believed were used by men to have sexual intercourse with underage girls. From the perspective of FLDS members like Nancy, however, the raid was unwarranted, and the disruption it caused to hundreds of lives was inexcusably cruel.

"The children would cry and hang onto their mothers," she recollected. "I get my strength from my Heavenly Father, but I can't believe something like this could even happen in America. . . . How could they take families and tear the children away?" Over the course of the next few months, Nancy would not be alone in expressing those sentiments.

On the one hand, Texas authorities and even former residents of the ranch applauded the government's seeming intolerance of sexual abuse. They reasoned that, while taking so many children into protective custody was undoubtedly traumatic, it was justified if it halted the victimization of underage brides. Yet for many FLDS members—as well as civil-liberties groups across the nation—the raid and the removal of minors from the ranch were more about persecution and prejudice than about protecting minors.

From their point of view, public misconceptions about polygamy and stereotypes that portrayed the FLDS as a backward religion were not sufficient reasons to rip apart hundreds of families. By May 2008 their perspective won added support when the Texas Supreme Court ordered that the overwhelming majority of youngsters be returned to their parents. Judges noted that authorities had failed to provide adequate evidence to warrant the children's removal in the first place. In the meantime, though, the raid on the

YFZ Ranch raised countless controversies and questions. Specifically, it prompted Americans to examine the complex and delicate relationship between guaranteeing religious freedom and simultaneously safeguarding child welfare.

Religious Freedom and Life at the Ranch

The right of U.S. citizens to practice whatever faith they choose is a critical part of the nation's heritage. As far back as colonial times, immigrants flocked to America in search of religious freedom. Several centuries later hundreds of distinct religious denominations claim followers within the country's borders.

In addition, the First Amendment to the U.S. Constitution guarantees that "Congress shall make no law respecting an establishment of religion, or prohibiting the free exercise thereof." This does not mean that it is acceptable for Americans to engage in an illegal activity simply because it corresponds to their religious beliefs. For example, the FLDS has come under scrutiny numerous times since it was founded in the 1930s, when certain Mormons decided to split from the Church of Jesus Christ of Latter-Day Saints (LDS).

One of the primary reasons for the separation was the LDS's views on plural marriage. Starting in 1890, church leaders formally banned polygamy—which is also illegal in all fifty U.S. states. Yet, while American legislators generally do not consider it acceptable for a man to have multiple wives, offenders are not always easily identified or consistently prosecuted. Many times they claim only one legally authorized marriage but still live with several women in what they consider "spiritual unions." Overall, government and law-enforcement officials tend to be most aggressive in

Polygamy, though illegal in the United States, still takes place. This Utah family consists of one father, three mothers, and twenty-one children.

singling out polygamists when they suspect child welfare is at stake.

For example, the most notable scandals involving the FLDS prior to the raid on the YFZ Ranch were rooted in cases of underage marriage or the sexual exploitation of minors. In the majority of U.S. states, citizens cannot be married until the age of eighteen or nineteen without some form of parental consent or court approval. Similar legislation also specifies how old an individual must be in order to legally consent to sexual intercourse. Though laws vary between states, the minimum age of consent is typically sixteen to eighteen. In Texas a person must be seventeen to legally engage in consensual sex. Citizens younger than eighteen cannot marry without special considerations, such as parental permission.

After the FLDS was created, its critics alleged that the church did not always abide by these rules. They accused leaders of condoning spiritual marriages that essentially forced underage girls into unions with older men the moment they reached puberty. One former FLDS member who claimed to have endured such circumstances noted how victims are frequently raised to unquestioningly marry whomever their parents and church officials deem appropriate — and at whatever age those adults consider acceptable. To disobey is to go against the wishes of the prophet, or the community's spiritual leader, even if the situation potentially involves rape, incest, teen pregnancy, or physical, sexual, or emotional abuse.

"We were just little girls . . . who thought we were going to hell if we didn't obey," remarked Laura Chapman, who fled a polygamous FLDS community in Arizona in 1991. "Who would think, right here in the United States of America, fathers are trading their daughters away like trophies? It's brainwashing and slavery. It's a complete system of organized crime right in our backyard that for some reason the government has simply chosen to ignore."

FLDS communities like the one in which Chapman was raised are sometimes referred to by outsiders as compounds.

They exist in Utah, Arizona, Texas, Colorado, South Dakota, and British Columbia. Often regarded by more mainstream portions of society as both intriguing and old-fashioned, the compounds are isolated from the surrounding world. It is common for women to style their hair in elaborate braids and to wear long dresses and skirts with high-buttoned blouses that seem in keeping with nineteenth-century fashions.

While modern technology does exist in these areas, innovations such as television and the Internet are not part of day-to-day life for most families. At the same time, however, many FLDS members have emphasized that their distinctions from mainstream America do not mean that every one of the approximately 10,000 individuals who belong to the church supports underage marriage. Nor do they all condone the abuses typically associated with it. For several, polygamy and other aspects of their existence promote core family values and religious principles they are confident will secure their place in a spiritual afterlife.

"Everyone talks about family values, but these people, they've really got family values," observed Scott Berry, a Utah lawyer who has represented the FLDS in the past. "They've got twenty to thirty children who've all got to get along. Money is always tight. They're more committed to family than anyone else I've seen in America." Regardless of this positive portrayal of FLDS members, even advocates of the religion admitted that the practice of polygamy had been at the center of several heated controversies by late 2003. And that fall—on the heels of these scandals—church leaders purchased land northeast of Eldorado to develop what ultimately became known as the YFZ Ranch.

FLDS communities live apart from mainstream America. One example of this can be found in the fashion and hairstyles of female church members.

Opposing Perspectives on Sister Wives

A woman who enters into a polygamist relationship often refers to her husband's other spouses as sister wives. For Americans who do not support the principles of plural marriage, it is difficult to imagine living in a marital union consisting of more than two people. Yet many practicing polygamists describe bonds with their sister wives as deeply fulfilling and defined more by mutual affection than jealousy.

"They're your sisters," explained a woman who asked to be referred to only as Ann and who admitted to being involved in a plural marriage in Centennial Park, Arizona. "You work together," she said in regard to her sister wives. "You genuinely care about each other." Not everyone shares Ann's perspective though.

"It takes a while to get over the jealousy," remarked one female polygamist. "You learn pretty fast to try to ignore what you're feeling." Another added, "I've seen women scratch, kick, [and] pull hair over how they load the dishwasher."

Five years after the FLDS purchased 1,700 acres of land near Eldorado in 2003, the property had been developed into an extensive community featuring a massive temple.

Innocent Community or Mysterious Cult?

When FLDS officials bought 1,700 acres of property in western Texas in November 2003, they immediately began developing the area. They claimed they were building a hunting retreat, but neighbors were suspicious. After the raid occurred in 2008, several people who owned nearby land came forward to tell reporters that the new residents "weren't very friendly" and, based on their manner of dressing and secretive behavior, appeared to belong to "some kinda cult."

As time passed, news started to spread that the ranch was populated by members of the FLDS and was intended to serve not as a hunting retreat but as a sprawling residential area. This information was supported by the emergence of several homes, gardens, and a meetinghouse, as well as silos,

Warren Jeffs appears in court in December 2006 on charges of sexual misconduct with a minor.

generators, a quarry, and a waste-treatment facility. Then, in 2005, a massive 90,000-square-foot limestone temple was erected on the property. While few outsiders were allowed regular access to the ranch, aerial photos led experts to believe that the structure towered about ten stories above the ground.

FLDS president Warren Jeffs, who was more commonly known as the religious group's prophet, dedicated the temple's foundation in January 2005. By the following June the state of Arizona issued a warrant charging him with two counts of sexual conduct with a minor and one count of conspiracy to commit sexual conduct with a minor. Authorities acted based on the testimony of FLDS members who had come forward with shocking stories that involved everything from forced marriage to sexual abuse. When Jeffs fled the area to avoid arrest, the federal government began pursuing him.

Authorities suspected that he may periodically have been hiding at the YFZ Ranch, but he was eventually captured in the summer of 2007. Within months, Jeffs was found guilty of acting as an accomplice to rape and was sentenced to ten years in prison. A judge determined that he had used his influence as a church leader to coerce a fourteen-year-old girl into consummating a spiritual marriage to her nineteen-year-old cousin.

Jeffs's ordeal heightened the intrigue and controversy surrounding the FLDS. Yet it was not the first scandalous episode involving the church to grab nationwide attention. In July 1953 state police and national guardsmen had entered an FLDS community known as Short Creek in what is present-day Colorado City, Arizona. Citing residents' disregard for antipolygamy laws, authorities arrested thirty-one men on charges related to bigamy—or having two spouses at the same time—and statutory rape. They also removed 263 children from their families. Many spent more than two years in foster care, and a handful were never returned to their parents' custody.

Unsurprisingly, the idea of children being torn away from their mothers and fathers did not sit well with a great number of Americans. Though much of the country regarded polygamy as an outdated and irregular practice, few U.S. citizens were as offended by the concept of plural marriage as they were by the image of babies being wrenched from their parents' arms. In addition, prosecutors were ultimately

Worries About Another Waco

The Short Creek raid was not the only example of what some Americans perceived as the government's overly aggressive attitude toward certain religious groups. In fact, the state of Texas was the site of an even more recent episode that pitted a unconventional sect against authorities. Between February 1993 and April 1993 the Bureau of Alcohol, Tobacco, Firearms, and Explosives (ATF), the Federal Bureau of Investigation (FBI), and the Texas National Guard were involved in a standoff with the Branch Davidians of Waco, Texas. Often described by outsiders as a cult, this group was an extremist offshoot of the Seventh-Day Adventist Church.

When authorities attempted to enter the Branch Davidians' property with a search warrant in early 1993 to investigate the sect's possession and handling of firearms and explosives, the situation rapidly

(continued)

deteriorated. Church members and law-enforcement officials exchanged gunfire, and a siege ensued that lasted fifty-one days and resulted in the burning of much of the Waco compound. In the end an estimated eighty-six people lay dead, and several others were wounded. Critics of the government alleged that authorities had displayed misconduct in firing at the Branch Davidians and might have contributed to the burning of their community. As suspicion surrounding Jeffs and the YFZ Ranch swelled more than a decade later, some individuals voiced the perspective that tensions between the state and the FLDS were setting the stage for another Waco.

"The possibility of another Waco . . . is huge," observed Jon Krakauer, the author of a book on Mormon extremism, in July 2005. "If [Jeffs] feels cornered and threatened, he will not go out alone; he has made that clear. He will not allow himself to be arrested. And [if the situation comes to a head] it is likely to happen in Texas."

unable to substantiate most of the allegations concerning polygamist unions and underage sex at Short Creek. This was primarily due to the fact that many of the births and marriages there had not been officially recorded.

In the end, critics of the raid likened it to a witch hunt and compared the government's treatment of FLDS members to its persecution of American Indians during the previous century. They complained that authorities had been overly aggressive and cruel in tearing apart hundreds of innocent families. People who sympathized with the church questioned whether officials had truly launched the raid to uphold laws that banned polygamy and protected children from abuse. Some suspected that they had instead acted out of their desire to uproot a religion they regarded as morally offensive.

U.S. citizens remained divided on the issue for the next five decades. From one perspective the FLDS gave the appearance of a secretive, peculiar cult that fostered convicted criminals such as Jeffs. The notion of child brides being raised in closed-off compounds and forced to submit to underage sex with much older husbands was disturbing to both average Americans and state and national authorities.

From another angle, though, FLDS members protested that this description was not typical of their lifestyle or beliefs. A few acknowledged that such scenarios undoubtedly occurred but attested that abuse was the exception to the rule and therefore did not justify the government's assault on their freedom of religion and individual liberties. These opposing vantage points made for mounting tensions that climaxed when a domestic-violence hotline in San Angelo, Texas, received a particularly disturbing phone call during the last weekend of March 2008.

Two

Overview
of the
Actual Raid

LOCAL AUTHORITIES AND CHILD PROTECTIVE SERVICES (CPS) officials working with the Texas Department of Family and Protective Services (DFPS) could not ignore the plight of Sarah Barlow. In March 2008 intake operators at a domestic-violence shelter in San Angelo, Texas, talked to a young woman who gave that name. She claimed she was a sixteen-year-old resident of the Yearning for Zion (YFZ) Ranch. Sarah insisted that she was being held against her will on property belonging to the Fundamentalist Church of Jesus Christ of Latter-Day Saints (FLDS) outside Eldorado, Texas. She indicated that she was a victim of sexual and physical abuse at the hands of her fifty-year-old husband, Dale Barlow. The caller told operators that she was pregnant and feared for her safety, as well as that of her eight-month-old infant.

What CPS workers didn't realize at the time was that "Sarah" was actually a mentally disturbed thirty-three-year-old named Rozita Swinton who was living in Colorado Springs, Colorado. Investigators would later discover that Swinton, who had no known ties to the YFZ Ranch, had a history of making similar phone calls to report false allegations of abuse. In March 2008, however, all they recognized was that a minor was pleading for protection—and that her story took place on FLDS property that had for a long time been shrouded in mystery and scandal. It had, after all, been less than a year since Warren Jeffs was sentenced for crimes that seemed to substantiate the type of lifestyle "Sarah" described as existing at the ranch.

In light of recent events and the gravity of the charges she was leveling, CPS officials and Texas Rangers felt they had little choice but to make their way to the YFZ compound. Swinton began placing her calls to the hotline in San Angelo in late March 2008, and by April 3, 2008, authorities were heading to the ranch. That evening, Schleicher County sheriff David Doran, two Texas Rangers, and what Doran described as "handful of officers went to the gate . . . with Child Protective Services and served a search warrant." They hoped to locate Sarah, her baby, Dale Barlow, and any records that offered evidence of his marriage to the girl or of their parenting a child together.

The sheriff later indicated to reporters that, though church leaders eventually made some effort to accommodate law-enforcement agents and CPS staff, they were not completely cooperative. Doran recalled "being held up at the gate for about two to three hours" after explaining their intentions to YFZ officials, who claimed they knew of no resident by the name Sarah Barlow. While authorities have argued that this delay was a stalling tactic by FLDS members, men and women living on the ranch say it was because the police failed to initially produce a warrant.

Whatever the actual scenario may have been, Texas Rangers, CPS employees, and local law-enforcement agents entered the gates shortly after 9:00 P.M. These individuals then set up operations at an on-site school, where child-welfare workers conducted interviews throughout the night. As time progressed, however, CPS officials grew increasingly dissatisfied with the speed at which the church was accommodating their requests to meet with sources in their hunt for Sarah. According to Doran the agency wanted to talk to a great number of girls, but FLDS members only ushered them into the school "in small increments through the night."

By April 4, 2008, each side of the investigation was becoming more impatient with and suspicious of the other. On the one hand, law-enforcement agents and CPS employees had started to grasp that the ranch was home to a far greater number of residents than they had been led to believe. Church leaders had initially told outsiders that about one hundred people lived on the property. After gaining entry to the ranch, though, police and child-welfare workers observed a much vaster population that was ultimately determined to be slightly more than seven hundred individuals.

Yet if authorities' distrust of FLDS members was mounting, so was ranch residents' apprehension about the men and women they perceived as intruders. Law-enforcement officials had called in officers carrying automatic weapons, K9 units, special weapons and tactics (SWAT) teams with snipers, helicopters, ambulances, and even an armored personnel carrier. They asserted that these measures were taken on a precautionary basis and were viewed more as backup than as resources intended for active use.

Nevertheless, the atmosphere at the ranch remained tense as April 4, 2008, wore on. And though authorities had

A Feeling of Being Unsafe

YFZ residents were not the only ones to express feelings of fear and uncertainty in the days following April 3, 2008. Several authorities also voiced concerns for their safety and a general uneasiness about how they would be treated. One CPS employee later noted how law-enforcement officials had hinted that she was in a somewhat precarious situation. The woman attested that it was not prudent to conduct house-to-house searches for children once the sun set.

She reported that police had advised her, "We are here to keep you safe, and we can't do that when it's dark." In addition, the investigator recalled FLDS men stationed at most building entrances and "heard there were men in trees with night-vision goggles." She ultimately summed up her perspective on working on the ranch by saying, "It's a feeling of being unsafe."

entered FLDS property with the intention of searching for Sarah and evidence of crimes committed against her, they had yet to locate the girl or her alleged husband. In fact, YFZ residents insisted that Barlow had not been present on the ranch for some time and actually lived in Arizona.

But CPS workers, Texas Rangers, and local police were not ready to give up their hunt based simply on the assertions of church leaders. They were well aware that Dale Barlow had pleaded no contest to charges of conspiracy to commit sexual conduct with a minor in 2007 and had subsequently been ordered to register as a sex offender. In addition, their observations of the men, women, and children who populated the ranch only made them more suspicious—and not just of Sarah's supposed husband.

Increased Tensions and a Mounting Investigation

According to Barbara Walther, judge for Texas's fifty-first district court, who would later become famous for her rulings in support of the raid, authorities had only been on FLDS property a short while before they came into "plain view . . . of additional criminal activity above and beyond what was alleged . . . including evidence of multiple instances of bigamy and sexual assault of additional children." The sight of several young mothers, as well as women they suspected were pregnant teenagers, prompted CPS and law-enforcement officials to intensify their investigation. They therefore began a residence-by-residence search and started collecting an assortment of evidence that was intended to prove far more than the reported abuse of a single YFZ teenager.

Judge Walther presided over custody hearings that determined the placement of the YFZ children.

Authorities obviously believed they were dealing with polygamy, underage sex, and other forms of criminal misconduct on a much broader scale than they had originally imagined. Complicating matters was their concern that FLDS families were hiding children by shuffling them from home to home as residential searches progressed. Investigators similarly suspected that parents were being intentionally uncooperative during interrogations and were withholding accurate information about whose children were whose.

From the perspective of YFZ residents, though, any hesitancy on their part wasn't unwarranted. They felt authorities were looking for excuses to trip them up and secure proof that they lived in polygamous households. FLDS members worried that the state was hunting for reasons to take their children away, and it wasn't long before their worst nightmares appeared to be coming true. On April 4, 2008—less than twenty-four hours after CPS, Texas Rangers, and local police had initiated the raid—authorities began removing children from the ranch.

"We're trying to find out if they're safe," explained CPS spokeswoman Marleigh Meisner. "We need to know if they have been abused or neglected." A coworker named Darrell Azar added that his agency had reason to suspect that eighteen of the minors in question "had been abused or were at immediate risk of future abuse." Authorities determined that it would be safer and more efficient to question the remainder of the children at an off-site location. Though investigators did not immediately release specific details about the evidence that substantiated their decisions, the removals continued on April 5, 2008.

By that point, authorities had taken 183 individuals from

the ranch, the majority of whom were girls. The children were temporarily housed at a civic center in Eldorado. Meanwhile, just as YFZ residents had begun to respond to the crisis of the removals, they watched in horror as a SWAT team burst through the doors of their towering limestone temple on April 5, 2008.

To FLDS members the intrusion was a terrifying and insulting violation of sacred grounds. They essentially regarded any outsider setting foot in the temple as a form of sacrilege. Church leaders pointed out that this is why they refused an initial request made by Texas Ranger captain Barry Caver to search the premises. As law-enforcement agents later testified, however, they had received evidence from a credible source about the building being used by men to have sex with underage girls as part of FLDS marriage rites.

After YFZ officials told Caver that his entering the temple would violate their religious beliefs, about fifty-seven residents formed a ring around the structure in an attempt to peacefully resist authorities. In the end, though, their efforts proved no match for SWAT team members who used a hydraulic tool called the Jaws of Life to open the building's doors on April 5, 2008. Fortunately, the maneuver did not result in violence, but an attorney for the church asserted that the invasion was a harrowing episode for already stunned and traumatized FLDS members.

Attorney Gerald Goldstein explained how residents of the ranch "were present and praying as officers drug them out of the way to gain entry to the temple. Officers were also observed firing weapons into the woods on the northwest corner of the temple as they entered. . . ." Court documents later revealed that, once inside, investigators found numerous locked safes, vaults, computers, and desks. Perhaps most damning, though, were their claims to have located an assortment of beds on the top floor of the temple—one of which allegedly contained a long strand of what appeared to be female hair.

The following day, authorities obtained a second search warrant that allowed their continued and more expansive scrutiny of the ranch. As boxes of evidence that investigators hoped would yield information related to marriages and births left FLDS property, so did numerous busloads of residents. By April 6, 2008, a total of 246 children and 93 women were transported from the ranch and the civic center in Eldorado to a larger shelter complex at Fort Concho in San Angelo.

In most cases mothers were allowed to accompany the youngsters if they so chose, but men were not permitted to leave the YFZ compound while the investigation was ongoing. Parents and church leaders—as well as CPS employees and law-enforcement officials—remained undeniably apprehensive as the rest of the search played out. For their part, FLDS members were understandably fearful of how their lives would be upturned next. And from the perspective of authorities, there was no way of predicting what further shocking secrets they would uncover.

Upheaval and Accusations

By April 7, 2008, more than 400 children had been removed from the YFZ Ranch, and 139 women had left the premises to accompany them to Fort Concho, which was rapidly nearing capacity. The FLDS had obtained twelve attorneys to represent its members, though only one member had been arrested since the raid began on April 3, 2008, on misdemeanor charges related to interfering with the state's investigation. Yet this incident was the least of YFZ residents' apparent worries. On April 7, 2008, Judge Walther ordered that all the children who had been removed from the ranch were to be officially placed in the state's temporary protective custody.

Over the next few days that edict was expanded to every child living on YFZ property. The official tally representing the total number of minors ultimately removed fluctuated and continues to be debated. This is partially due to the fact that authorities were frequently unable to refer to birth certificates and were not always confident they were receiving accurate information about children's ages from parents. As a result, some FLDS members that investigators originally assumed were teenagers were later found to be adults. A report released by CPS lists the final number of minors taken into custody as 439, but other sources indicate it was greater than 460.

After the raid occurred, mothers were initially permitted to stay with their children at Fort Concho. Eventually, additional shelters in the San Angelo area were used to house the overwhelming number of former ranch residents. Within a week of the raid, investigators and CPS employees left the YFZ compound, and Judge Walther announced that a subsequent hearing would be held on April 17, 2008. She indicated that she would then reevaluate the situation based on evidence that had been collected and determine whether the FLDS children should remain in state custody.

In the meantime the media scrambled to gather interviews and capture a picture of what life was like at the YFZ Ranch

Feelings of Victimization at Fort Concho

Many FLDS mothers felt their rights continued to be violated as they were brought to Fort Concho with their children. They deeply resented the fact that Judge Walther had ordered their cell phones confiscated on April 13, 2008, in an effort to prevent witness tampering. In addition, the perspective of FLDS mothers that they were the target of state persecution was only strengthened by what they perceived as the poor conditions inside the Texas shelter. Several complained that their living quarters were so crowded that playpens, cribs, and cots were shoved side-by-side. Women noted that this atmosphere had proven a source of stress for the children, whom they claimed were frequently ill and suffering from a variety of gastrointestinal complaints.

"You would be appalled," mothers predicted in a letter to Texas governor Rick Perry in mid-April 2008, when they pleaded with him to intervene on their behalf. "Many of our children have become sick as a result of the conditions they have been placed in. Some have even had to be taken to the hospital. Our innocent children are continually being questioned on things they know nothing about. The physical examinations were horrifying to the children. The exposure to these conditions is traumatizing them."

An FLDS mother breaks down in front of reporters while discussing separation from her children.

before, during, and after the raid. Newspapers, magazines, and prime-time television all displayed photographs of sobbing mothers and the massive white temple that stretched ten stories above the reclusive polygamist community. With these images as a backdrop, FLDS members who agreed to speak to reporters typically repeated a common theme—that they were upstanding citizens and decent parents who simply wished to practice their religion in peace.

Many spoke of "the privilege of worshiping God as guaranteed by the Constitution." Other YFZ residents emphasized that "We are not child abusers. . . . These are innocent and sweet children. The only abuse [the] children have ever had is since they've been taken away."

Intermingled with these arguments were the protests of FLDS lawyers who posed various questions about the legality of the search warrants law-enforcement officials had used to scrutinize the ranch. They also debated whether a holy place such as the temple should have had greater immunity from investigation. Ultimately, attorneys for the church conceded to the authority of the state on several of these issues.

Yet they were also quick to point out that police and CPS still had not succeeded in locating the teenage caller who had sparked the raid in the first place. As of mid–April 2008 investigators had failed to positively identify Sarah and her baby among the hundreds of minors who had been placed in state custody. As for her supposed husband, all accounts appeared to support Barlow's claim that he had no connection to a girl by that name and was not even living in Texas.

From the perspective of the men and women who supported the raid and removal of YFZ children, however, Sarah's case—whether legitimate or not—was representative of hundreds of other situations involving abuse. Her phone calls had led investigators to uncover what they believed was a hotbed of polygamist activity, underage sex, and systematic brainwashing. To law-enforcement officials and CPS employees, the events of early April 2008 were not so much about violating FLDS members' freedom of religion as they were about protecting children.

"There is a pervasive pattern and practice of indoctrinating and grooming minor female children to accept spiritual marriages to adult male members of the YFZ Ranch, resulting in them being sexually abused," noted CPS investigator Lynn McFadden. "This pattern and practice places all of the children located at the YFZ Ranch, both male and female, to risks of emotional, physical, and/or sexual abuse." In the days to come, these risks were among the reasons several individuals gave to justify authorities' decision to separate FLDS youngsters from their families.

Three
Voices Supporting the State

IN THE WAKE OF THE RAID on the Yearning for Zion (YFZ) Ranch, Americans across the nation listened to law-enforcement officials and employees with Child Protective Services (CPS) explain why their actions had not been overly aggressive. Yet it was one thing for these individuals to emphasize that the placement of 439 children who were members of the Fundamentalist Church of Jesus Christ of Latter-Day Saints (FLDS) into temporary state custody was rooted in child welfare and not religious persecution. It was quite another to hear this assertion come from the lips of women like former church member Carolyn Jessop.

Jessop had chronicled her break from the FLDS and her departure from a polygamist community in Colorado City, Arizona, in a best-selling book titled *Escape*. At the age of eighteen she had become the fourth wife of Merril Jessop, an FLDS leader who essentially headed the ranch in Eldorado, Texas, at the time of the raid. After having eight children with him, however, Carolyn—who shared a home with six other women who claimed forty-six sons and daughters of their own—fled in 2003.

Carolyn Jessop testified before a congressional committee in 2008 about crimes associated with polygamy.

She later recounted her abusive relationship with Merril and how deciding to leave him was a perilous move. If she had been caught attempting to escape, Carolyn believed, her children would have been taken from her and she would have been regarded as an outcast by the FLDS community. As Carolyn observed to reporters once she had safely abandoned polygamy and had subsequently been granted a divorce and parental custody, women in her culture were taught to endure arranged marriages. Girls were groomed to become wives who practiced silent obedience, even if that virtue concealed a lifetime of physical, emotional, and sexual torment.

"I was born in the United States, and I never experienced the bounty of a free life," she noted. "The [FLDS] . . . doesn't consider abuses against women a crime. However, it does consider a woman talking about abuse a crime." When authorities raided the YFZ Ranch five years after Carolyn had moved away from Merril and the oppressive existence she described, she applauded their efforts.

"Texas is not going to be a state that's as tolerant of these crimes as Arizona and Utah have been," she said. "In Eldorado, the crimes went to a whole new level. They thought they could get away with more." Based on statements made by some of the young women interviewed at the ranch, Carolyn's claims did not seem unfounded.

Many women insisted they had not been abused and enjoyed happy, tranquil lives grounded in family values. But Tom Green County district attorney Stephen Lupton revealed that some of the girls authorities questioned appeared to be teenage mothers who did not even know their own age. In a particularly striking episode, one such source was asked how old she was, which prompted her husband to inform her, "You are eighteen." The young woman then reportedly "parroted" her spouse's response. In light of the stories former FLDS members such as Carolyn shared following the raid, however, brainwashing and a lack of self-knowledge were only a few of the dilemmas girls living on the YFZ Ranch likely faced.

"In the FLDS, women are not supposed to show affection to their children," Carolyn remarked. "It's conferring value on an individual, and only the prophet and the head of the family are allowed to do that. I have heard people say they think it's cruel that children have been separated from their mothers because of the raid on the Texas compound. But that's a projection of an attached and loving relationship. . . . Most children attach to another child for survival and protection like children do in orphanages." On the heels of the raid, Carolyn reaffirmed her conviction that a hellish cycle of abuse was being overturned by the authorities' work in Eldorado. To support her perspective, she shared a particularly painful example from her own relationship with Merril.

"The worst abuse in [our] family was a technique he called 'breaking,'" she recollected. "He would slap a baby until it screamed and then hold it under running water. The baby would choke and scream, and he'd torture the infant again. This happened to one of my sons. I was pregnant at the time and completely terrorized by what I was seeing. I knew if I intervened, Merril would punish me and possibly hurt my baby even more. Evil is coming undone in Texas, and I am overjoyed."

Acting in the Children's Best Interest

From every indication, CPS workers and law-enforcement officials agreed with Carolyn's sentiments. On April 11,

2008, authorities unveiled eighty-eight pages of documentation listing items they had seized during the raid on the YFZ Ranch. Computer equipment, journals, photo albums, family Bibles, personal letters, and school and medical records were among their collection of evidence.

While FLDS members decried investigators' confiscation of their personal possessions as intrusive and unwarranted, CPS employees, police, and Texas Rangers said that their actions were justified. They reiterated to the media time and again that they had not conducted the raid as part of a religious witch hunt. Nor, emphasized CPS spokesman Darrell Azar, was his agency out to persecute YFZ residents simply because certain aspects of their faith did not dovetail with the customs and beliefs of mainstream Americans.

"You can worship what you want, think what you want," he said. "But if you act to abuse girls sexually in Texas, we are going to take action." Affidavits that Judge Barbara Walther allowed to be unsealed in the week following the raid gave the impression that such wrongdoing was indeed occurring. Sworn statements by Schleicher County sheriff David Doran, Texas Ranger sergeant Brooks Long, and other law-enforcement officials and CPS staff provided accounts of several pregnant teens and young mothers on the ranch.

In addition, Doran reported that an informant had confessed how the beds located in the YFZ temple were where "males over the age of seventeen engage in sexual activity with female children under the age of seventeen." Describing life at the ranch as a "very volatile situation," CPS spokeswoman Marleigh Meisner defended her agency's decision to do whatever was necessary to prioritize child welfare.

"What we did was warranted and in the best interest of the children," she told reporters. "This is not about religion—this is about keeping children safe from abuse." Helping the public understand this vantage point was particularly important in the wake of the raid, especially as FLDS mothers began to criticize the state's treatment of their families. Many complained of being denied access to their children and of suffering in overcrowded conditions within shelters in San Angelo, Texas.

In an effort to provide former YFZ residents with less cramped living quarters, CPS employees transported the majority of them to the San Angelo Coliseum on April 14, 2008. Yet not everyone was permitted to remain at the new shelter. From the perspective of child-welfare officials as well legal professionals and mental-health experts, it was best to temporarily separate mothers who had joined their children after their removal from the ranch. Exceptions were made for women with sons and daughters aged four or younger. The remainder of adult FLDS mothers were given the option of returning to the Eldorado compound.

Meanwhile, approximately two dozen of the teenage boys who had been taken from the YFZ property were placed at Cal Farley's Boys Ranch in Amarillo, Texas. Children were dispersed to other area shelters as well, including the Wells Fargo Pavilion in San Angelo and the Seton Home in San Antonio, Texas. Naturally the tearful farewells said by so many mothers, sons, and daughters made for a sight that many people considered painful to behold. For FLDS women the parting was a renewed exercise in separation and upheaval, not to mention what they considered inexcusable treatment at the hands of CPS officials and Texas authorities.

An FLDS mother expresses her frustration and despair while staying at a San Angelo shelter.

Unsurprisingly individuals from this latter group offered an excuse—and some insight into their point of view, which they noted was not shaped by cruelty or hard-heartedness.

"It is not the normal practice to allow parents to accompany the child when an abuse allegation is made," explained CPS spokeswoman Marissa Gonzales. And with suspicions of widespread sexual abuse heading up what was quickly evolving into Texas's largest child-custody case, the agency deemed it unwise to leave the majority of YFZ minors in their mothers' care. From their vantage point they could not afford to readily trust women who belonged to a culture that—per the testimony of Carolyn and others like her—fostered everything from religious brainwashing to statutory rape. Naturally some child-welfare officials also felt that any interviews they conducted with FLDS children would be less inhibited in their parents' absence. As April 17, 2008, approached, men and women on both sides of the controversy surrounding the raid anxiously prepared to see if that absence would be prolonged by Judge Walther's ruling.

Perspectives That Shaped a Judge's Position

On April 17 and April 18, 2008, attorneys for both the state and FLDS members presented their arguments in the Tom Green County Courthouse in San Angelo. Legal counsel for YFZ residents emphasized that justification for the raid was weak and that a handful of pregnant teenagers was not in and of itself evidence of abuse. More to the point, they accused Texas officials of seeking to persecute the FLDS church and of wanting to put the religion itself on trial.

No One Left Untouched

Despite some Americans' perspective that CPS was exacting a cruel and unusual punishment in advocating the separation of so many FLDS mothers from their children, the agency insisted that it was anything but hard-hearted. From their point of view, such measures were called for, even if they were emotionally difficult for everyone involved. As Azar admitted, "Separating women from children is always a difficult thing. There were tears by the children, by the women, and by some of our caseworkers as well. It's not easy to do, and no one was untouched." He was also quick to point out, however, that the separation was "the only alternative at this time."

A FLDS parent leaves the Tom Green County Courthouse in the company of her attorney.

Witnesses ranging from theological experts to mothers who lived on the ranch took the stand. They testified that underage marriages were generally not encouraged within their faith—and especially not since Warren Jeffs had ceased to act as their leader. They stated time and again that the FLDS culture was not defined by abuse or activities that posed a threat to children. Yet some of the women who resided on the YFZ compound also conceded that underage marriages did, in fact, occur. Several witnesses called by the state took this admission a step further.

"There is a culture of young girls being [made] pregnant by old men," said CPS investigator Angie Voss, who interviewed ranch residents during the course of the raid. She went on to testify that, based on her observations and experiences, it was reasonable to conclude that "more than twenty girls, some of whom are now adults, have conceived or given birth under the age of sixteen or seventeen." Bruce Perry, a psychiatrist who had studied children in the context of cults, offered a similar perspective when he took the stand.

Describing the FLDS belief system as "abusive," he also asserted that "the culture is very authoritarian." By April 18, 2008, Perry and numerous other experts expressed their opinions to Judge Walther during twenty-one hours of testimony. The details of each FLDS child's specific circumstances were not addressed.

Walther estimated that giving every individual case five minutes of consideration and courtroom debate would result in approximately seventy hours of deliberation. As she promised on April 18, 2008, the YFZ children and their families would ultimately be entitled to personalized state attention. In the meantime, though, she felt she had to make a more immediate decision regarding their welfare. She therefore prepared to issue a temporary ruling despite FLDS members' complaints that they were being denied due process, or the basic rights associated with standard courtroom procedures.

Walther noted, "The issue before the court is: Can I give them back?" Onlookers—including a great number of FLDS parents—displayed little emotion as she explained on April 18, 2008, that she believed the answer to that question to be no. She stated that the children would continue to remain in state custody temporarily as the court and CPS

A Psychiatrist's Standpoint

Though Perry described the YFZ Ranch as a setting that most definitely put several children at risk of abuse, his vantage point was also shaped by a cautionary tone. He conceded that "there are parts of what they [FLDS members] do that are very destructive." Yet he explained that, based on his observations, many aspects of life at the compound appeared to be rooted in love and what most Americans regarded as wholesome family values.

When Perry was asked whether he considered all the children to be in equal danger, he acknowledged that he "lost sleep over that question." He told the court that he believed babies and toddlers to be in a somewhat less precarious position than older girls. The psychiatrist added, however, that even younger children would ultimately be subject to the same religious concepts and practices that had piqued CPS officials' suspicions in the first place.

No matter which minors were at the greatest risk of abuse, though, Perry advised Walther that the situation required special cultural sensitivities. Specifically he was against the idea of placing YFZ children in traditional foster care. Perry emphasized that thrusting young FLDS members into mainstream society, which they had previously been sheltered from, was bound to be "destructive." He therefore urged the court to develop individualized care plans that aimed to teach the children free will and independent thought while taking into consideration the environment in which they had been raised.

investigators evaluated each individual case. The judge also declared that a subsequent hearing would be held on or before June 5, 2008. At that time she would review the status of the children as well as that of the investigation into the alleged abuses occurring at the YFZ Ranch.

Walther made few other comments when she handed down her ruling, except to say that it was her duty to ensure that the minors in question were provided with a "safe environment." Based on her decree that they stay in the hands of the state, she was obviously not convinced that the YFZ Ranch met this specification. From the perspective of CPS workers and several psychological and child-welfare experts, Walther's decision was a sound one.

To them the removal of hundreds of children was validated by the notion that the FLDS community had stood by while youngsters suffered abuse or stood at risk of being subjected to it. In the minds of the men and women who supported the raid, the case was not simply about a handful of pregnant teenagers. It was about scores of young girls being raised to believe that underage sex and polygamous marriages represented a normal way of life.

So even if CPS investigators conceded that they had no evidence of infant or preteen girls enduring abuse, children from these groups were not safe by virtue of the values that the FLDS promoted. Child-welfare officials likewise noted that boys who had formerly resided on the ranch were in a precarious position as well. They were essentially being reared to become future perpetrators—men who would ultimately take on underage brides with the blessing of church leaders.

Yet Walther and her advocates recognized that mere suspicions of an abusive environment at the ranch were not sufficient to keep children from their parents. The state needed hard, cold evidence to flesh out the details of each child's situation. The judge therefore ordered DNA studies and fingerprinting in order to establish family ties. Since she and other authorities felt that FLDS members had often been less than forthcoming about which child belonged to which mother, they were hopeful that testing would provide definitive answers. With clearly established bloodlines laid out before the court, there could be no question about who was the offspring of an underage parent.

In the meantime, CPS started arranging for the minors to be placed in foster care and boys' and girls' homes throughout the state. Mothers who were nineteen and older were permitted to stay with youngsters four and younger until DNA testing was complete. After that point the age cutoff at which the FLDS women would be allowed to remain with their children indefinitely would drop to eighteen months.

Unsurprisingly the decision was a difficult blow for most FLDS parents. Apart from being devastated by the destruction of their community and families, church members had a far different perspective on the raid than state officials and CPS investigators. From the vantage point of these individuals, religious persecution played just as great a role in their misery as the loss of their children.

Four
Perspectives of the Persecuted

"THEY WERE WRONG when they kicked in the gate. . . . They were wrong when they brought in the guns and they ordered the children at gunpoint on the buses. . . . They were wrong when they raided [the ranch] with a false and fake allegation to get into the place. . . . Where do you wanna stop saying it was wrong. . . . People are presumed innocent. Where's the presumption of innocence here?" So spoke Willie Jessop, a representative of the Fundamentalist Church of Jesus Christ of Latter-Day Saints (FLDS), as he offered reporters his take on the raid several weeks after it occurred.

His version of events differed slightly from the one given by Child Protective Services (CPS) officials and the state. While authorities proclaimed that they were evaluating every FLDS child's situation on a case-by-case basis and had tried to create as many smooth transitions as possible for families, most Yearning for Zion (YFZ) Ranch residents heartily disagreed. From the perspective of church members such as Jessop, CPS investigators presented a flimsy case

Willie Jessop defends the beliefs and rights of YFZ residents to reporters.

at best—and one that hardly warranted the upheaval of an entire community.

"Do you want me to go into your community and gather up everybody in your city streets?" he asked one reporter. "And do you want the government to have your DNA on your daughter and your children and your family for what purpose? To try to come up with some perverted allegation against you?"

When the news correspondent answered Jessop's hypothetical inquiries by reminding him that the circumstances he was describing stemmed from allegations of sexual abuse, the church leader bristled. As he explained, FLDS families felt that they were being unfairly persecuted by the state.

After all, his church was not the only one in America to have been at the center of similar controversies.

"So [have] the Catholics, so has any other religion, including Mormons," Jessop noted, listing religions that have been involved in abuse scandals. "Should we just take them all down? Is there not a crime committed in any religion? Why do we single [Mormons] out?"

In response, several FLDS members speculated about various reasons their faith was being targeted. They theorized that when mainstream Americans looked at their culture, they primarily saw women in old-fashioned prairie dresses with elaborately braided hair. They fixated on men with multiples wives and families who didn't own television sets because they didn't want to expose their children to excessive sex and violence. Though most YFZ residents conceded that these distinctive elements did shape life at the ranch, they did not mean that their church was evil or abusive.

"We're being persecuted," remarked one FLDS father whose children had been taken during the raid and who asked that the media identify him only as Richard. "That's the way we feel. There's a quote from the apostle Paul that I like: 'He who lives godly in Christ Jesus will be persecuted for his religion.'"

From the vantage point of FLDS parents like Richard, there were few other words besides "persecution" to describe the reason for their suffering. They watched helplessly as their children were funneled through the state's foster-care system and inundated by mainstream American culture, which they had never been exposed to at the ranch. When FLDS mothers had been permitted to stay with the youngsters in

An Appeal to the President

Jessop was determined that his perspective on the raid reach far beyond the ears of Texas officials. In fact, he headed straight to the top of the U.S. government with a letter directed to President George W. Bush that was delivered on May 10, 2008. In addition to encouraging the president to intervene on behalf of the FLDS, it included a request for him to visit the YFZ Ranch in person.

"Patriotism is shown when elected officials are willing to stand up and defend the Constitution," Jessop noted in his correspondence. "We are not asking them to agree with the beliefs of an unpopular religion, but to defend human rights that have been violated by these unprecedented terrorist acts." While Bush never took Jessop up on his invitation to tour the ranch, the highly publicized letter helped the FLDS spokesman express his opinion that "the freedom of every man, woman, and child is under attack."

San Angelo, Texas, immediately following the raid, they had complained of cramped, overcrowded conditions.

At least, however, they were able to care for and comfort their families. But then in mid-April 2008 women were ordered to leave children who were more than eighteen months old after DNA testing was complete. Faced with another traumatic separation experience, FLDS parents shuddered at reports that their sons and daughters were distraught and pleading for their parents.

One member of the church, who admitted that she was involved in a polygamous relationship, said she understood why the state had to take rumors of abuse seriously. Yet she objected to allegations that applied to only a handful of individuals being used to justify the mass removal of children from their mothers and fathers. "If there is abuse, that should be investigated and taken care of," she said. "But I do not see how you can use that to justify taking 416 children out of their homes and away from their families."

Opinions on Investigators' Evidence

From the vantage point of YFZ residents, authorities and CPS officials had failed to produce any evidence that justified the removal of minors from the ranch. For starters, in late April 2008 law enforcement had linked thirty-three-year-old Rozita Swinton of Colorado Springs, Colorado, to the disturbing calls supposedly placed by Sarah Barlow in March of that year. Swinton herself had never been a member of the FLDS but did have a history of making fake abuse allegations.

The state reacted to this information by saying that Swinton's calls had ceased to serve as the backbone of their case against the church. By April 28, 2008, CPS employees announced that, regardless of Swinton's involvement, they still had thirty-one girls in their custody who were younger than seventeen and who were either pregnant or had already had children. In addition, they revealed that they had several reports of children on the ranch suffering from an inordinate number of bone fractures. And, of course, there was the unsettling fact that a series of beds had been located on the top floor of the YFZ temple during the raid.

Yet FLDS leaders and church attorneys fired back at the state by asserting that all of these factors could be reasonably explained and were not in and of themselves evidence of widespread sexual abuse. For example, they argued that children who lived on the ranch often had medical histories that featured hereditary bone disease. Combined with their active lifestyles, this fact reduced the strength of any argument that broken bones were conclusive proof of youngsters being abused.

As for the beds in the temple, FLDS officials scoffed at allegations that they were part of sexual rites involving underage girls and disregarded the state's theory as both ridiculous and demented. They instead suggested that they were probably used either by a groundskeeper or by church members who needed to rest during lengthy ceremonies that sometimes included fasting. From the vantage point of YFZ residents, even the CPS's claim that it had custody of underage mothers was not particularly powerful evidence.

"Let's put it this way," reasoned Jessop. "Has any member in society had sex with underaged girls?" Surely, he and other FLDS members rationalized, a few incidents of wrongdoing were not enough to subject an entire community to the loss of its children. Just as important, they said that the absence of official records such as birth certificates had probably prompted authorities to take into custody people who they assumed were children but who were actually adults. In light of these arguments, residents of the ranch complained bitterly that the state had no real reason to have invaded their lives. They insisted that the actions of CPS officials, police, and Judge Barbara Walther offered substantial proof that officials were targeting their faith and violating their right to freedom of religion.

By the end of April 2008 no official charges of statutory rape or child abuse had been filed against residents of the ranch in connection to the raid. At the same time, however, FLDS parents started preparing to appeal Judge Walther's decision in the hope that their sons and daughters would be returned. From their point of view, this was one of the few solutions left to them as their families were subjected to DNA testing, interrogations, and intense emotional turmoil. As these men and women began the process of taking on CPS and the state of Texas, they discovered that several civil-liberties groups and legal professionals shared their perspectives on the raid.

Outside Vantage Points Opposing the State

Initially the Texas Third Court of Appeals refused to consider a plea made by forty-five FLDS mothers to halt the "scattering of [their] children" throughout the foster-care system. Yet YFZ residents took heart in the realization that they were not alone in their dissatisfaction with the state. As evidence of this fact, attorneys from Texas RioGrande Legal

Aid (TRLA)—a nonprofit organization that provides free legal services—offered their assistance to the FLDS families.

On April 30, 2008, lawyers from TRLA filed another appeal on behalf of the YFZ mothers. They did not insist that the state drop its investigation into the abuse allegations or unquestioningly return all the children to the ranch. Instead they requested that male YFZ residents be allowed to leave the Eldorado property. This way, mothers could be reunited with their children and head back to the ranch in the absence of any men that CPS and the state considered potential perpetrators of sexual abuse. Alternately, TRLA attorneys suggested that women be provided with an offsite location where they could at least remain in the company of their sons and daughters.

"This case is not about whether [the state] is entitled to investigate allegations of child abuse," the petition stated. "This case is about whether [the state] may deprive mothers of possession of their children without evidence that the mothers pose an immediate physical danger to the children."

TRLA lawyers and their clients took exception to how Judge Walther had made a single mass ruling, as opposed to making the time to evaluate each child's circumstances on an individual basis. They similarly objected to the way in which authorities were treating the several households within the ranch as being part of one larger home situation. Attorneys noted that it was dangerous to assume that just because hundreds of people resided in the same community, they shared identical values and beliefs. They argued that not every married couple at YFZ was involved in a polygamous relationship. TRLA staff also insisted that it was not practical to accuse all FLDS members of supporting sexual abuse simply because a small percentage of people who practiced that religion showed evidence of being underage mothers.

"The department [CPS] cannot take the circumstance of less than 5 percent of the children and extrapolate to over 400 children at the ranch," they observed. "In short, to remove a child from his mother, there has to be individualized proof as to that mother." TRLA attorneys did not believe that the state could offer such evidence.

Without it, a growing number of Americans were adopting the perspective that the raid more resembled a religious witch hunt than an organized effort to promote child welfare. And as of early May 2008, it appeared that organizations such as the American Civil Liberties Union (ACLU) had a similar take on the events. The group released the following statement on May 2, 2008:

> Law enforcement officials have . . . removed
> every child who was living at the ranch . . .
> and the state has justified that decision . . .
> by explaining that all children at the ranch
> were at risk because they were exposed to
> FLDS beliefs regarding underage marriage.
> Religion is never an excuse for abuse. But,
> exposure to a religion's beliefs, however
> unorthodox, is not itself abuse and may not
> constitutionally be labeled abuse.

In addition, the ACLU emphasized that "state officials have an important obligation to protect children against abuse. However, such actions should not be indiscriminately targeted against a group as a whole—particularly when the

Willie Jessop (center) talks with CPS caseworkers upon their return to the ranch on May 21, 2008.

group is perceived as being different or unusual. Actions should be based on concrete evidence of harm and not based upon prejudice against religious or other communities."

As May 2008 wore on, people with this vantage point entered into increasingly heated debates with Americans who felt the state was justified in doing whatever was necessary to potentially protect children from sexual abuse. Meanwhile, DNA testing continued, as did authorities' interrogation of YFZ families. San Angelo officials estimated that the raid and the demands it placed on social services and law-enforcement agencies were costing Texas millions of dollars.

CPS investigators admitted to the strain of having to wade through volumes of evidence that had been confiscated in early April 2008. On May 21, 2008, they returned to the ranch on the suspicion that residents were hiding yet more children there. This time, however, FLDS members were able to refuse authorities entry because they lacked a search warrant. The day before, CPS had been forced to admit that four of the women it had originally taken into custody as minors were actually adults. Due to the lack of official documentation and what investigators perceived as an absence of forthright cooperation from FLDS parents, they said that it was not unreasonable for this mistake to have occurred.

With such errors looming over the raid and the controversies that had arisen in its wake, Americans waited to see what the Third Court of Appeals would rule on May 22, 2008. Would judges overturn or uphold Walther's decisions? Would they essentially decide that the raid was representative of how easily an American's right to religious freedom could be violated? Or would the court agree with Walther that an entire community's belief system was sufficient to pose a threat to its children?

Another State's Take on Events in Texas

From the perspective of several officials in Utah and Arizona, Texas authorities had acted rashly and in a manner that they did not intend to replicate in their own states. Such areas also had histories that featured Mormon polygamy. Yet, according to local leaders such as Utah attorney general Mark Shurtleff, they did not approve of Texans' logic in tearing apart so many families.

"Let's say you're a six-month-old girl, no evidence whatsoever of any abuse," he explained. "They're [CPS officials] simply saying, 'You, in this culture, may grow up to be a child bride when you're fourteen. Therefore we're going to remove you now when you're six months old.' Or, 'You're a six-month-old boy . . . forty years from now you're going to be a predator, so we're going to take you away now.'"

Five
Opinions on Long-Term Implications

A FEW MONTHS AFTER AUTHORITIES had knocked on the gates of the Yearning for Zion (YFZ) Ranch, the child-custody case that had captured national attention was presented to a new set of judges. And as the public discovered on May 22, 2008, justices serving the Third Court of Appeals in Austin, Texas, had their own perspectives on events that had transpired in early spring of that year. Much to the joy of parents belonging to the Fundamentalist Church of Jesus Christ of Latter-Day Saints (FLDS), who had endured separation from their children and what they insisted were unfair allegations of abuse, judges declared that Child Protective Services (CPS) officials and Judge Barbara Walther had been wrong.

"The Department [CPS] did not present any evidence of danger to the physical health or safety of any male children or any female children who had not reached puberty," they noted in their ruling. "Nor did the Department offer any evidence that any . . . pubescent female children were in physical danger other than that those children live among a group of people who have a 'pervasive system of belief' that condones polygamous marriage and underage females having children.

The existence of the FLDS belief system . . . by itself, does not put children of FLDS parents in physical danger. It is the imposition of certain alleged tenets of that system on specific individuals that may put them in physical danger."

In other words, certain elements of YFZ residents' faith—no matter how odd or offensive some people considered them to be—were not sufficient to warrant authorities' removal of hundreds of children from the ranch. The court of appeals ruled that CPS needed to provide hard evidence for each child that proved he or she was being physically harmed or was at immediate risk of suffering physical harm. From the justices' point of view, child-welfare officials had failed in this capacity, and Judge Walther had "abused [her] discretion" by not returning the youngsters to their parents. They ordered her to restore the children to their rightful families within ten days of their decision, made on May 22, 2008.

In response, CPS wasted little time contesting the ruling, and within a week, the case had been brought before Texas's state supreme court. The end result, however, was the same. On May 29, 2008, justices announced that they were "not inclined to disturb the court of appeals' decision." Members of the state supreme court further elaborated "On the record before us, removal of the children was not warranted."

Key players who had been involved in the raid inevitably had mixed reactions to the ruling. CPS officials admitted that they were disappointed, but they pledged that they would do their utmost to uphold the state supreme court's decision. Representatives of the agency also took heart in the realization that it did not mean they had to abandon their investigation into the YFZ Ranch. The ruling simply reinforced the idea that they needed to find evidence of abuse on

Dissenting Opinions About Dangers to Children

While six of the nine Texas Supreme Court justices voiced their complete support of the idea that YFZ children should be immediately returned to their families, the remaining three dissented. Despite the fact that the majority ruled, a handful of justices believed that the state's actions had not been completely unwarranted. They conceded that perhaps the boys who had been removed from the ranch were not at any real risk of being abused. These justices could not definitively say the same, though, when it came to pubescent girls, whom Justice Harriet O'Neill described as being "demonstrably endangered."

a case-by-case basis in order to place children into protective custody.

"We understand and respect the court's decision and will take immediate steps to comply," a statement released by CPS read. "Child Protective Services has one purpose in this case—to protect the children. Our goal is to reunite families whenever we can do so and make sure the children will be safe." Unsurprisingly not everyone who advocated for the raid and the subsequent removal of FLDS minors from the ranch was as accepting of the justices' ruling. Barbara Elias-Perciful, an attorney representing children's interests, shared her frustration with reporters.

"This case involves the systematic rape of minor children—conduct that is institutionalized and euphemistically called 'spiritual marriage,'" she emphasized. "Typically, there is no media coverage of the horrific acts sexual predators commit against children . . . if the media showed the actual events of adult males demanding sex with eleven-year-old girls, there would be no one questioning the graphic danger of returning these children to their home at this time." Naturally YFZ residents disagreed with this interpretation. Just as important, though, they applauded what they perceived as the court's efforts to end the state's persecution of their church.

"You cannot wipe out an entire community in an entire town over an allegation that's so blanketed," observed FLDS spokesman Willie Jessop. "I mean it's like, 'Let's take out every Catholic because we don't like their practice or there may be some wrongdoing.' But you can't take out a whole community. . . . We hoped that that would not happen and we're very grateful that here in America, it didn't happen."

From the Vantage Point of a Polygamy Expert

Following the raid, some individuals expressed the opinion that FLDS members actually stood to benefit from what they described as persecution. "Mormon polygamists need devils more than they need gods," remarked John Llewellyn, a former law-enforcement agent and the author of books such as *Polygamy's Rape of Rachael Strong*. He is widely accepted as an expert on Mormon polygamy.

"They portray themselves as perpetual victims—underdogs," Llewellyn continued during a 2010 interview. "At the same time, they want the 'religious freedom' to brainwash and oppress females so they can cultivate harems. . . . The religious aspect is a facade that provides the 'falsified' justification to cultivate the ego by establishing dominance over women and pursuing sex with many wives."

Backlash Brought on by the Raid

By early June 2008 the overwhelming majority of children who had been removed from YFZ that April were returned to the ranch. Exceptions included a young teenager who the state concluded had been married to Warren Jeffs when she was just twelve. Though many FLDS parents living on the compound were ordered to attend parenting classes and sign agreements promising to protect their families from abuse, the upheaval of the raid at last seemed at an end. Yet could the images of the temple being invaded and mothers being separated from their sobbing youngsters be buried in the past? Just as important, could Americans forget the idea of child brides in outdated prairie dresses being handed over to much older husbands as an expression of the FLDS faith?

The long-term implications of the raid stretched far beyond the immediate trauma that families had experienced and the shock with which the public had reacted to accounts of polygamy and underage sex. And just as the events of April 2008 had prompted varied opinions and perspectives, so did the question of whether the aftershock of the state's clash with the FLDS had set the stage for positive change. Not everyone agreed that it had.

"Bigotry and all this animosity, it's really creeping up," noted Marvin Dockstader, a member of a church called the Work of Jesus Christ, which split from the FLDS about three decades ago. "It's hypocritical. America was created by people running from that." Dockstader and other residents of a polygamist community in Arizona known as Centennial Park expressed their concerns to reporters after the dust from the raid on the YFZ Ranch had settled.

A YFZ mother rejoices at being reunited with her children in June 2008.

They took little reassurance in the fact that several Arizona legislators indicated they were interested in prosecuting polygamists only when sexual abuse was alleged or child welfare was at stake. As Dockstader explained, he didn't attribute persecution of his religion to state officials. He was more wary of what he termed "the mob"—members of the American public who had scarce knowledge of or tolerance for certain aspects of his faith.

Nor were Dockstader and other U.S. citizens who practiced polygamy alone in suffering from the social pressures and anxieties they perceived as a being a direct result of the YFZ raid. Politicians and authorities in states such as Utah and Arizona also grumbled about the ill effects of the Eldorado incident. In addition to having to fend off accusations that, compared with Texan officials, they were soft on sexually abusive polygamists, they struggled to maintain open relationships with local FLDS communities. As Arizona attorney general Terry Goddard pointed out, effective communication with fundamentalist religious groups was essential for recognizing and eliminating potential threats to child welfare.

"We've done a lot to establish trust and a lifeline," he remarked of his state's efforts to reach out to such sects. "If suspicion and hostility reasserts itself, we may get cut off. If it works out well, we'll be able to at least do some damage control and make it clear that Utah and Arizona aren't Texas." Utah attorney general Mark Shurtleff elaborated on how the mistrust local FLDS members felt toward the government on the heels of the YFZ raid potentially jeopardized child welfare in certain situations. He observed that in some cases, victims of sexual misconduct were more reluctant to come forward or press charges for fear that CPS officials and police would take drastic actions and uproot their entire community.

"They want us to punish the guy who hurt them or the guy who ordered it, either Warren Jeffs or their husband," Shurtleff said. "They don't want their whole family impacted. They still love their siblings." Yet Shurtleff's perspective was by no means universal. While the raid undoubtedly heightened tensions and insecurities for some Americans on the subject of how much protection they truly had from religious persecution, it was a stepping stone for others.

Perceptions of Positive Effects

One of the leading arguments used by people who opposed the actions of the state at the YFZ Ranch was that it was unfair to assume everyone in the FLDS was an abuser. Several church members conceded that polygamy did exist in Eldorado and even admitted that underage marriages had possibly occurred. But they repeatedly emphasized that child brides and forced unions were not a standard of normalcy there.

Regardless of how rare ranch residents proclaimed such circumstances to be, it was difficult for Americans to lose sight of the seriousness of the allegations. From the perspective of these citizens the raid was therefore not a total mistake. Starting in July 2008, Schleicher County prosecutors began indicting twelve FLDS members—including Jeffs and Merril Jessop—on sexual-abuse charges. As they handed down a total of twenty-six indictments during the next five months, Texas authorities declared that this aspect of the raid's aftermath was evidence that it had been warranted.

"The indictment seems to indicate CPS was correct in its belief that some children at the ranch had been sexually abused, and all children are at risk in a community in which adults do not take a stand against the abuse taking place in their homes," noted CPS spokesman Patrick Crimmins. The charges, which included sexual assault of a child, bigamy, conducting an unlawful marriage ceremony involving a minor, tampering with evidence, and failing to report abuse, stemmed largely from evidence that had been collected during the raid.

To date, three of the twelve indicted FLDS members have been convicted. Yet from the vantage point of certain

Texas attorney general Greg Abbott looks toward photos of FLDS members indicted on sexual abuse charges.

individuals, bringing sexual abusers to justice was only one positive effect that society realized in the aftermath of the raid. As former church member Flora Jessop explained, the events of April 2008 also raised public awareness about what she perceived as evils associated with the FLDS and polygamy. Backing up her theory was a final CPS report released in late 2008 indicating that the agency believed nearly two-thirds of YFZ families had children it considered victims of abuse or neglect.

"I think the nature of the abuse and the severity of the abuse is going to shock people," Jessop predicted when discussing criminal trials involving FLDS members that were taking place in October 2009. As protestors and spectators routinely offered their opinions outside the courthouse in San Angelo, Texas, that fall, Jessop was proven partially right. Many average Americans were appalled by the idea of pregnant teenagers bearing children for older men whom they recognized as their spiritual husbands in polygamous relationships. Others, though, condemned the government's efforts to overshadow people's individual religious principles.

"God designed us to have children at that age," one picketer who supported the accused observed of FLDS girls who had reached puberty but were too young to engage in consensual sex under Texas law. "Our Congress knows better than God," he added with sarcasm. But not every person present at the courthouse shared the perspective that religious freedom should supersede laws that safeguard child welfare.

"I object to their religion," proclaimed a woman who had been watching the trials. "I object to a religion that exploits women and children—even though there is freedom of religion." For better or worse, these clashing vantage points exemplified another positive outcome of the raid. The story that had begun unfolding on April 3, 2008—and that continues to play out to this day—forced Americans to consider both the power and the priorities of the government. Was it more important to do all that was necessary to protect children or to exercise greater caution so that citizens' cherished civil liberties would be upheld? Just as significant, people started pondering if there was some way for key players on both sides of the raid to work together in the future so that neither effort was jeopardized.

Six

Looking at the YFZ Legacy

A YEAR AFTER THE RAID on the Yearning for Zion (YFZ) Ranch, Americans wondered whether life had returned to normal in Eldorado, Texas. From the look of things, the compound belonging to the Fundamentalist Church of Jesus Christ of Latter-Day Saints (FLDS) was relatively calm and quiet once more. At the very least, it was not the scene of chaos and crisis it had been approximately twelve months before. Nonetheless, memories of April 2008 still haunted YFZ residents, whose perspectives on coping with the countless emotions they had experienced since that time were varied. For some such as James Dockstader, who is a father of four, anxiety that Texas authorities would conduct another raid continued to be overwhelming a year later.

"It's a hell," he admitted in the spring of 2009. "Our peace is looking beyond, [to] the Heavenly Father." Yet other FLDS parents were just as moved by bitterness and anger as they were by fear and uncertainty. Church member Lamar Johnson expressed his fury at a particularly painful recollection involving his young son.

"He celebrated his first birthday at Fort Concho," Johnson said. "Somebody owes me for that." His sentiments

Moving Ahead from Young People's Perspectives

In the spring of 2008, Americans were confronted with photographs and video footage of distraught mothers and children who faced the anxiety of separation and uncertain futures. Naturally such images were hard for many people to get out of their minds, even a year after authorities first set foot on the YFZ Ranch. It therefore made sense that the public continued to be interested in the stories and perspectives of perhaps the most important players in the raid—the FLDS children who ultimately returned to the Eldorado compound. When interviewed by reporters in March 2009, some youngsters appeared confident and unafraid that CPS would interfere with their families a second time.

"We live by faith," declared twelve-year-old

Joseph Barlow. "We don't live by fear. We know everything they [the authorities] say are lies. You don't have to believe in lies." Yet not all the children expressed the same self-assurance.

"I couldn't cry," confessed fourteen-year-old Kloe Barlow of her reaction to being separated from her family. Like a great percentage of her peers, she had tried to regain as much normalcy as possible in the months following the raid, but it was a difficult effort. A year after she had first been brought to the schoolhouse to be interviewed by CPS officials, Kloe still refused to sit in the chair where she had waited to speak to officials that evening. "It hit me so hard, I didn't cry for a long time."

Like the YFZ residents shown here, most FLDS families were reunited a few months after the raid took place. Nonetheless, many continue to struggle with the trauma they experienced in the spring of 2008.

were not unique among YFZ residents. Many lamented the dramatic disruption to their families' lives and its subsequent effects on their children, whom parents frequently described as moodier and less able to concentrate following the raid. Several also complained that personal effects ranging from college diplomas to photographs still had not been returned by investigators who had confiscated them as evidence in April 2008.

While the majority of FLDS members bristled at what they remembered as ill treatment by the state, some emphasized that they believed the worst was behind them. "We're grateful [the children are] here and doing as well as they are," one mother remarked. "Life will get better."

An Unapologetic Point of View

Despite the fact that the majority of YFZ residents felt it would take a while to recover from authorities' actions the previous April, CPS officials offered few apologies or regrets. In fact, many observed that they would not hesitate to repeat their actions. A year later they continued to insist that their motives had always been rooted in promoting the interests of American children and had absolutely nothing to do with persecuting people because of their religious beliefs.

"Given the exact fact situation, we would go in again and remove the children," said agency spokesman Patrick Crimmins. "We responded to a report that we believed to be authentic. . . . We were obligated under Texas law to investigate." Anne Heiligenstein, commissioner of the Texas Department of Family and Protective Services (DFPS), supported this point of view and added that FLDS children were better off because of the state's efforts.

"Today girls at the ranch know that a 'spiritual marriage' is sexual abuse," she stated on the one-year anniversary of the raid. "They know how to report abuse. And they know that if they call, someone will come, someone will listen, and someone will help them. They now have a voice. . . . The environment that children returned to is safer than the one they left."

Some critics, however, have questioned the practicality of Heiligenstein's sentiments. They point out that a great percentage of YFZ residents resent CPS and will not abandon their anger and mistrust anytime soon. For Heiligenstein, though, this does not mean that FLDS leaders will not demonstrate heightened awareness and a more proactive attitude when it comes to their moral responsibilities toward children.

"They're [FLDS members] taking pretty seriously the risk of the state of Texas intervening again," she said. "This organization knows that if they're living in Texas, they'll take the laws of Texas very seriously from now on." There is little doubt that key players involved in the YFZ raid will continue to reflect on the event itself and the impact it had from a wide array of perspectives for decades to come. Yet the state and the FLDS need to coexist in American society. They must therefore find methods of working together that both embody a spirit of religious tolerance and advocate for the welfare of U.S. children.

Balancing Key Issues Involved in the Raid

Though YFZ residents and state authorities may never see eye to eye on every angle of the 2008 raid, each side has subsequently taken steps to better balance some of the primary issues at stake. For example, the FLDS has officially denounced underage marriages. While church leaders always insisted that they were not commonplace on the ranch, several YFZ sources had hinted at their periodic occurrence. Instead of shrugging off criticism, spokesman Willie Jessop said the FLDS was formally outlining its opposition to the practice.

"The church is clarifying its policy on marriage," he explained. Jessop added that, moving forward, FLDS leaders would "neither request nor consent" to spiritual unions involving underage girls. Though CPS took note of this stance, some of its staff expressed the opinion that YFZ residents' actions would ultimately speak louder than their words.

"Only time will tell if they honor that pledge," remarked Heiligenstein on behalf of CPS. "But they certainly know without a doubt that Texas will not idly stand by while they sexually abuse young girls." Heiligenstein went on to elaborate how her agency had not closed the book on the ranch just because the children had been reunited with their parents. She pointed out that CPS workers were determined to collaborate with families to create open channels of communication and to foster community education.

"Many people think the CPS cases ended when the children returned to their families," she observed. "They did not. We continued to work with those families—especially

Breaking Down Barriers

The Utah-Arizona Safety Net Committee is one example of ways Americans representing different backgrounds and interests unite to ensure that citizens can enjoy religious freedom without sacrificing child welfare. Members of the organization, which was formed in 2003, work together so that "people associated with the practice of polygamy have the same educational opportunities and access to justice, safety, and services as the general public." Men and women affiliated with the group aim to promote "open communication, break down barriers, and accomplish these original goals: provide training and develop materials for public awareness; reduce isolation, secrecy, abuses of power, and crime; and find ways to provide access and education to members of polygamous communities."

Unsurprisingly the effectiveness of Safety Net was put to the test in the aftermath of the raid. Yet many people remain optimistic that Americans on all sides of the various issues involved will continue to utilize the organization and others like it. "It [the raid] might even tighten the groups," said one worker involved with a nonprofit group that strives to aid survivors of abuse within polygamous relationships. "The polygamists attend to break down the barriers and build the bridges. It might help. Maybe we'll get more participation."

the mothers and teen daughters. Parents . . . know that turning a blind eye to sexual abuse puts their family at risk. The girls attended classes where we explained what sexual abuse is and how to report it."

Outside of Eldorado, Americans in general have also taken additional steps to find the ideal balance between preventing this type of abuse and preserving religious freedom. Town hall meetings, *National Geographic* specials, and even Home Box Office (HBO) dramas have set the stage for discussions surrounding expressions of faith—such as polygamy—that don't dovetail with mainstream culture or the law. The perspectives of the U.S. citizens who converse and often debate about these topics cover a broad spectrum of beliefs.

Despite this diversity, many people maintain the vantage point that honest and open communication between Americans with different opinions is critical to helping society understand and accept religious groups that are far from mainstream. It allows members of such faiths to explain their beliefs and dispel what they consider to be common public misconceptions. In turn, authorities are able to evaluate child welfare in a manner that is based more on reliable information and facts than on allegations and stereotypes. Ideally, increased dialogue and cooperative efforts between sects such as the FLDS and state agencies such as CPS will prevent another large-scale raid. Some church members hope that being at the center of so much public attention will have the same effect as well.

"My sister was on *Larry King*," remarked YFZ mother Nancy Barlow about a year after the raid. "I hope they [the public] notice we're people, and glad to be alive and glad to be home." Regardless of whether Barlow's hopes are ultimately fulfilled, Americans will undoubtedly continue to have clashing perspectives on the best ways to support freedom of religion while promoting child welfare. What is certain is that the 2008 raid had a powerful impact on U.S. society in the context of both these issues.

Timeline

1890   Leaders within the Church of Jesus Christ of Latter-Day Saints (LDS) formally ban polygamy.

1930s   Some Mormons split from the LDS to form the Fundamentalist Church of Jesus Christ of Latter-Day Saints (FLDS).

July 1953   State police and national guardsmen enter an FLDS community in what is present-day Colorado City, Arizona, and arrest thirty-one men on charges related to bigamy and statutory rape. They also remove 263 children from their families during what becomes known as the Short Creek raid.

February 1993   Authorities begin a standoff with the Branch Davidians of Waco, Texas, that lasts through April 1993 and results in an estimated eighty-six deaths.

November 2003   FLDS officials buy 1,700 acres outside Eldorado, Texas, to house what eventually becomes recognized as a polygamous community called the Yearning for Zion (YFZ) Ranch.

January 2005   FLDS prophet Warren Jeffs dedicates the foundation of the towering limestone temple on the YFZ Ranch.

June 2005   Authorities issue a warrant charging Jeffs with two counts of sexual conduct with a minor and one count of conspiracy to commit sexual conduct with a minor; he is captured a few years later and is convicted in the fall of 2007.

Late March 2008 Intake operators at a domestic-violence hotline in San Angelo, Texas, receive calls from a female they believe to be an FLDS member named Sarah Barlow. Claiming to be a YFZ resident, the caller alleges abuse at the hands of her much older husband, with whom she is involved in a polygamous relationship.

April 3, 2008 Child Protective Services (CPS) agents and law-enforcement officials enter the YFZ Ranch outside Eldorado with a search warrant to look for Sarah and evidence that she has been abused.

April 4, 2008 CPS workers begin removing children from the ranch.

April 5, 2008 By this point, authorities have taken 183 individuals from the ranch, the majority of whom are girls. In addition, they forcibly enter the FLDS temple to search for evidence of abuse.

April 6, 2008 Authorities obtain a second search warrant to justify their continued and more expansive search of the ranch. As of this date, 246 children and 93 women have been transported away from the YFZ property.

April 7, 2008 More than 400 children have been removed from the YFZ Ranch, and 139 women have left the premises to accompany them to off-site CPS housing. Barbara Walther, judge for the fifty-first district court, orders that the children be temporarily placed in the state's protective custody.

April 13, 2008   Judge Walther orders that the cell phones of FLDS women staying at Fort Concho in San Angelo be confiscated in order to avoid witness tampering; YFZ mothers write to Texas governor Rick Perry complaining about conditions within the state's shelter system.

April 14, 2008   The majority of YFZ minors are transported from Fort Concho to other area shelters, including the San Angelo Coliseum. For the most part, only women with sons and daughters aged four or younger are allowed to stay with their children.

April 17, 2008   Judge Walther hears attorneys representing both the state and FLDS members offer arguments about the welfare of the YFZ children. On April 18, 2008, she rules that the minors will continue to remain in state custody temporarily as the court and CPS investigators evaluate each individual case. She also orders fingerprinting and DNA testing to establish definitive family ties and evidence of possible sexual abuse. At this time, it is decided that mothers who are nineteen and older will be permitted to stay with youngsters four and younger until DNA testing is complete. After that point, the age cutoff at which the FLDS women will be allowed to remain with their children indefinitely will drop to eighteen months.

April 28, 2008   CPS employees announce that they have thirty-one girls in their custody who are younger than seventeen and are pregnant or already have children.

April 30, 2008   Lawyers with Texas RioGrande Legal Aid (TRLA) file an appeal with the Texas Third Court of Appeals on behalf of the YFZ mothers.

Late April 2008   Law-enforcement officials link thirty-three-year-old Rozita Swinton of Colorado Springs, Colorado, to the disturbing calls supposedly placed by Sarah Barlow in March.

May 2, 2008   The American Civil Liberties Union (ACLU) issues a formal statement in regard to the raid indicating that a person's religious beliefs alone are not sufficient to accuse an individual of abuse.

May 10, 2008   YFZ spokesman Willie Jessop delivers a letter to President George W. Bush asking him to intervene on behalf of the FLDS.

May 21, 2008   CPS officials return to the ranch on the suspicion that residents are hiding yet more children there. This time, however, FLDS members are able to refuse authorities entry because they lack a search warrant. The day before, CPS was forced to admit that four of the women it had originally taken into custody as minors were actually adults.

May 22, 2008   Justices with the Texas Third Court of Appeals rule that the state lacked sufficient evidence to remove children from the YFZ Ranch and order that they be returned to their families. CPS makes plans to appeal this decision to the Texas Supreme Court.

May 29, 2008   Justices serving the state supreme court uphold the court of appeals' ruling.

June 2008   The overwhelming majority of children who had been removed from YFZ the previous April are returned to the ranch.

July 2008   Schleicher County prosecutors begin indicting twelve FLDS members—including Jeffs and Merril Jessop—on sexual abuse charges. They hand down twenty-six indictments during the next five months that are rooted in accusations that include sexually assaulting a child, committing bigamy, conducting an unlawful marriage ceremony involving a minor, tampering with evidence, and failing to report abuse.

Late 2008   CPS releases a final report indicating that the agency believes nearly two-thirds of YFZ families have children it considers victims of abuse or neglect.

Notes

Chapter One

p. 9, "Original Mormons": terminology used by members of the FLDS, quoted in B. A. Robinson, "FLDS Intro: Terminology, Overview & Organization," *Religious Tolerance*, July 25, 2004, www.religioustolerance.org/ fldsintro.htm (accessed March 2, 2010).

p. 9, "Fundamentalist Mormons": terminology used by members of the FLDS, quoted in B. A. Robinson, "FLDS Intro: Terminology, Overview & Organization."

p. 10, "[They] didn't give us an . . .": Nancy, quoted in Nancy Perkins and Brian West, "First Look Inside YFZ Ranch," *The Deseret News*, April 13, 2008, www. deseretnews.com/article/1,5143,695270108,00. html?pg=2 (accessed March 2, 2010).

p. 10, "poked [his] face into . . .": Nancy, quoted in Nancy Perkins and Brian West, "First Look Inside YFZ Ranch."

p. 10, "give me that baby!": Nancy, quoted in Nancy Perkins and Brian West, "First Look Inside YFZ Ranch."

p. 14, "had been abused or . . .": CPS officials, quoted in Bill Kirkos, "137 Children Removed from Polygamist Ranch," *CNN*, April 5, 2008, www.cnn.com/2008/ CRIME/04/04/texas.ranch/ (accessed March 2, 2010).

p. 14, "The children would cry . . .": Nancy, quoted in Nancy Perkins and Brian West, "First Look Inside YFZ Ranch."

p. 15, "Congress shall make no law . . .": verbiage of the First Amendment of the U.S. Constitution, "Introduction to the Establishment Clause," *University of Missouri-Kansas*

City School of Law: Exploring Constitutional Conflicts, date
originally published not available, www.law.umkc.edu/
faculty/projects/ftrials/conlaw/estabinto.htm (accessed
March 2, 2010).

p. 17, "We were just little girls . . .": Laura Chapman,
quoted in Susan Greene, "Polygamy Prevails in Remote
Arizona Town," *Help the Child Brides*, March 4, 2001,
www.helpthechildbrides.com/stories/laurachap.htm
(accessed March 2, 2010).

p. 18, "Everyone talks about family values . . .": Scott
Berry, quoted in Susan Greene, "Polygamy Prevails in
Remote Arizona Town."

p. 20, "They're your sisters . . .": Ann, "Sister Wives
Describe Bright Side of Polygamy," *The HOPE
Organization*, March 2, 2006, www.childbrides.org/
CPAC_Primetime_sister_wives_describe_bright_side_
of_polygamy.html (accessed March 6, 2010).

p. 21, "It takes a while . . .": female polygamist #1, quoted in
Susan Greene, "Polygamy Prevails in Remote Arizona
Town."

p. 21, "I've seen women . . .": female polygamist, #2, quoted
in Susan Greene, "Polygamy Prevails in Remote
Arizona Town."

p. 22, "weren't very friendly": neighbors of YFZ
residents, quoted in Peter Van Sant, "The YFZ
Ranch," *CBS*, May 27, 2008, www.cbsnews.com/
stories/2008/05/27/48hours/main4130161.shtml
(accessed March 2, 2010).

p. 22, "some kinda cult": neighbors of YFZ residents, quoted in Peter Van Sant, "The YFZ Ranch."

p. 26, "The possibility of another . . .": Jon Krakauer, quoted in Jordan Smith, "Meet the New Neighbors," *The Ross Institute Internet Archives for the Study of Destructive Cults, Controversial Groups and Movements*, July 29, 2005, www.rickross.com/reference/polygamy/polygamy367.html (accessed March 6, 2010).

Chapter Two

p. 29, "handful of officers went . . .": David Doran, quoted in Ben Winslow, "News Interview with Schleicher County Sheriff David Doran of Texas," *The Deseret News*, June 4, 2008, www.deseretnews.com/article/700231719/News-interview-with-Schleicher-County-Sheriff-David-Doran-of-Texas.html?pg=1 (accessed March 2, 2010).

p. 29, "being held up at . . .": David Doran, quoted in Ben Winslow, "News Interview with Schleicher County Sheriff David Doran of Texas."

p. 30, "in small increments through . . .": David Doran, quoted in Ben Winslow, "News Interview with Schleicher County Sheriff David Doran of Texas."

p. 31, "We are here to keep . . .": CPS employee, quoted in Matt Phinney, "Live from the Courthouse: Updates on FLDS Custody Hearing," *Free Republic*, April 17, 2008, www.freerepublic.com/focus/f-news/2003172/posts (accessed March 6, 2010).

p. 31, "heard there were men . . .": CPS employee, quoted

in Matt Phinney, "Live from the Courthouse: Updates on FLDS Custody Hearing."

p. 31, "It's a feeling of . . .": CPS employee, quoted in Matt Phinney, "Live from the Courthouse: Updates on FLDS Custody Hearing."

p. 32, "plain view . . . of additional . . .": Barbara Walther, quoted in MyEldorado.net, "Judge Rules YFZ Evidence Admissible at Trial," *The HOPE Organization*, October 8, 2009, www.childbrides.org/holdem_ES_judge_rules_YFZ_evidence_admissable_at_trial.html (accessed March 2, 2010).

p. 34, "We're trying to find out . . .": Marleigh Meisner, quoted in Bill Kirkos, "Possible Standoff Looms at Polygamist Ranch," *CNN*, April 5, 2008, www.cnn.com/2008/CRIME/04/05/texas.ranch/index.html (accessed March 2, 2010).

p. 34, "had been abused or were . . .": Darrell Azar, quoted in Bill Kirkos, "Possible Standoff Looms at Polygamist Ranch."

p. 35, "were present and praying as . . .": Gerald Goldstein, quoted in Bill Hanna, "Temple Used for Sex with Young Girls, Officials Say," *Star-Telegram*, April 9, 2008, www.star-telegram.com/2008/04/09/572931/temple-used-for-sex-with-young.html (accessed March 2, 2010).

p. 39, "You would be appalled . . .": FLDS mothers, "Polygamous Sect Moms Appeal to Texas Governor," *CBS4*, April 13, 2008, cbs4denver.com/national/polygamist.sect.mothers.2.698762.html (accessed March 6, 2010).

p. 41, "the privilege of worshipping God . . .": YFZ
residents, quoted in David Von Drehle, "The Texas
Polygamist Sect: Uncoupled and Unchartered," *Time*,
April 24, 2008, www.time.com/time/magazine/article/
0,9171,1734818,00.html (accessed March 2, 2010).

p. 41, "We are not child abusers . . .": YFZ residents,
quoted in Nancy Perkins and Brian West, "First Look
Inside YFZ Ranch."

p. 42, "There is a pervasive pattern . . .": Lynn McFadden,
quoted in Paul A. Anthony, "More Victims, State Says
After Interviewing All Sequestered Children from
YFZ Ranch," *The Standard-Times*, April 9, 2008, www.
gosanangelo.com/news/2008/apr/09/more-victims-state-
says-after-interviewing-all (accessed March 2, 2010).

Chapter Three

p. 45, "I was born in the United States . . .": Carolyn
Jessop, quoted in Jordan Muhlestein, "Ex-Polygamist
Wife Talks About Her Experiences," *The HOPE
Organization*, October 22, 2005, www.childbrides.org/
carolyn_StdE_Carolyn_talks_about_her_experiences.
html (accessed March 2, 2010).

p. 45, "Texas is not going to be . . .": Carolyn Jessop,
quoted in Ben Winslow, "Hildale and Colorado City
Worry over Texas Raid," *The Deseret News*, April 5, 2008,
www.deseretnews.com/article/1,5143,695267615,00.
html?pg=1 (accessed March 2, 2010).

p. 45, "You are eighteen": words of YFZ husband as

remembered by Stephen Lupton, quoted in Ben Winslow, "Texas Fights Challenge to FLDS Evidence," *The HOPE Organization*, September 19, 2008, www.childbrides.org/raid_des_Texas_fights_challenge_to_YFZ_evidence.html (accessed March 2, 2010).

p. 46, "parroted:" Stephen Lupton, quoted in Ben Winslow, "Texas Fights Challenge to FLDS Evidence."

p. 46, "In the FLDS, women . . .": Carolyn Jessop, "Woman Learns to Be a Mother Outside FLDS," *The HOPE Organization*, May 11, 2008, www.childbrides.org/carolyn_azcent_learns_to_be_a_mother_outside_FLDS.html (accessed March 2, 2010).

p. 46, "The worse abuse in . . .": Carolyn Jessop, "Woman Learns to Be a Mother Outside FLDS."

p. 47, "You can worship what . . .": Darrell Azar, quoted in Miguel Bustillo and Nicholas Riccardi, "Texas Has Its Own View of Polygamists," *The Los Angeles Times*, April 12, 2008, www.articles.latimes.com/2008/apr/12/nation/na-compound12 (accessed March 2, 2010).

p. 47, "males over the age of seventeen . . .": David Doran, quoted in Paul A. Anthony, "Teen Girls from YFZ Ranch Near Eldorado Have Multiple Children, Affidavits Disclose," *The Standard-Times*, April 10, 2008, www.gosanangelo.com/news/2008/apr/10/teen-girls-from-yfz-ranch-near-eldorado-have/ (accessed March 2, 2010).

p. 48, "very volatile situation": Marleigh Meisner, quoted in Paul A. Anthony, "Teen Girls from YFZ Ranch Near Eldorado Have Multiple Children, Affidavits Disclose."

p. 48, "What we did was . . .": Marleigh Meisner, "ACLU Weighs in on Texas Polygamist Custody Case," *CNN*, April 20, 2008, www.cnn.com/2008/CRIME/04/20/ polygamy.sect/ (accessed March 2, 2010).

p. 50, "It is not the normal . . .": Marissa Gonzales, quoted in Scott Michels, Mike Von Fremd, Kelly Hagan, and Jonann Brady, "Polygamist Moms Return to Ranch," *ABC*, April 14, 2008, www.abcnews.go.com/GMA/ story?id=4646965&page=1 (accessed March 2, 2010).

p. 51, "Separating women from children . . .": Darrell Azar, "Sect Children from YFZ Ranch All in Foster Care," *CNN*, April 25, 2008, www.cnn.com/2008/CRIME/04/25/ polygamy/index.html (accessed March 2, 2010).

p. 51, "the only alternative at . . .": Darrell Azar, "Sect Children from YFZ Ranch All in Foster Care."

p. 53, "There is a culture of . . .": Angie Voss, quoted in Kirk Johnson and John Dougherty, "Sect's Children to Stay in State Custody for Now," *The New York Times*, April 19, 2008, www.nytimes.com/2008/04/19/us/19raid. html (accessed March 2, 2010).

p. 53, "more than twenty girls . . .": Angie Voss, quoted in Kirk Johnson and John Dougherty, "Sect's Children to Stay in State Custody for Now."

p. 53, "abusive": Bruce Perry, quoted in the Associated Press, "One Witness Calls Sect Harmless, Another Calls It Abusive," *Fox*, April 18, 2008, www.foxnews.com/ story/0,2933,351753,00.html (accessed March 2, 2010).

p. 53, "the culture is very . . .": Bruce Perry, quoted in the

Associated Press, "One Witness Calls Sect Harmless, Another Calls It Abusive."

p. 53, "The issue before the court . . .": Barbara Walther, quoted in the Associated Press, "One Witness Calls Sect Harmless, Another Calls It Abusive."

p. 54, "there are parts of what . . .": Bruce Perry, quoted in the Associated Press, "One Witness Calls Sect Harmless, Another Calls It Abusive."

p. 54, "lost sleep over that . . .": Bruce Perry, quoted in the Associated Press, "One Witness Calls Sect Harmless, Another Calls It Abusive."

p. 55, "destructive": Bruce Perry, quoted in the Associated Press, "One Witness Calls Sect Harmless, Another Calls It Abusive."

p. 56, "safe environment": Barbara Walther, quoted in Kirk Johnson and John Dougherty, "Sect's Children to Stay in State Custody for Now."

Chapter Four

p. 58, "They were wrong when . . .": Willie Jessop, quoted in Peter Van Sant, "The YFZ Ranch."

p. 59, "Do you want me to . . .": Willie Jessop, quoted in Peter Van Sant, "The YFZ Ranch."

p. 60, "So [have] the Catholics . . .": Willie Jessop, quoted in Peter Van Sant, "The YFZ Ranch."

p. 60, "We're being persecuted . . .": Richard, quoted in Nancy Perkins and Brian West, "Life's Tough for FLDS Man Without Family," *The Deseret News*, April 13,

2008, www.deseretnews.com/article/695270113/Lifes-
tough-for-FLDS-man-without-family.html (accessed
March 2, 2010).

p. 61, "Patriotism is shown when . . .": Willie Jessop,
quoted in Nancy Perkins, "Letter Asks Bush to Help
FLDS Kids," *The Deseret News*, May 11, 2008, www.
deseretnews.com/article/1,5143,700224855,00.html
(accessed March 6, 2010).

p. 61, "the freedom of every . . .": Willie Jessop, "Letter to
President George W. Bush," *Truth Will Prevail*, May 11,
2008, www.truthwillprevail.org/index.php?parentid=1&
index=7 (accessed March 6, 2010).

p. 62, "If there is abuse . . .": FLDS member, quoted in
Gary Tuchman and Amanda Townsend, "A Dark
History Repeats for Religious Sect," *CNN*, April 11,
2008, www.cnn.com/2008/CRIME/04/10/polygamist.
towns/index.html (accessed March 2, 2010).

p. 63, "Let's put it this way . . .": Willie Jessop, quoted in
Peter Van Sant, "The YFZ Ranch."

p. 64, "scattering of [their] children . . .": verbiage of plea
made by FLDS women to the Texas Third Court
of Appeals, "Timeline of Raid of FLDS-Owned
YFZ Ranch," *The Deseret News*, May 28, 2008, www.
deseretnews.com/article/1,5143,700228439,00.
html?pg=3 (accessed March 2, 2010).

p. 65, "This case is not about . . .": verbiage of second
petition by FLDS women to the Texas Third Court of
Appeals, quoted in Brian West, "FLDS Women Petition

to Have Kids Returned," *The Deseret News*, May 1, 2008, www.deseretnews.com/article/695275333/FLDS-women-petition-to-have-kids-returned.html?pg=1 (accessed March 2, 2010).

p. 66, "The department [CPS] cannot take . . .": verbiage of second petition by FLDS women to the Texas Third Court of Appeals, quoted in Brian West, "FLDS Women Petition to Have Kids Returned."

p. 66, "Law enforcement officials have . . .": verbiage of statement issued by the ACLU, "ACLU Statement on the Government's Actions Regarding the Yearning for Zion Ranch in Eldorado, Texas," *The ACLU*, May 2, 2008, www.aclu.org/religion-belief/aclu-statement-governments-actions-regarding-yearning-zion-ranch-eldorado-texas (accessed March 2, 2010).

p. 66, "state officials have an . . .": verbiage of statement issued by the ACLU, "ACLU Statement on the Government's Actions Regarding the Yearning for Zion Ranch in Eldorado, Texas."

p. 69, "Let's say you're a . . .": Mark Shurtleff, quoted in Ben Winslow, "Utah, Arizona AGs Feel Fallout from FLDS Raid," *The Ross Institute Internet Archives for the Study of Destructive Cults, Controversial Groups and Movements*, May 4, 2008, www.rickross.com/reference/polygamy/polygamy897.html (accessed March 2, 2010).

Chapter Five

p. 70, "The Department [CPS] did not . . .": verbiage of decision made by the Texas Third Court of Appeals, "No.

03-08-00235-CV," *The Texas Third Court of Appeals*, May 22, 2008, www.3rdcoa.courts.state.tx.us/opinions/html opinion.asp?OpinionId=16865 (accessed March 2, 2010).

p. 71, "abused [her] discretion": verbiage of decision made by the Texas Third Court of Appeals, "No. 03-08-00235-CV."

p. 71, "not inclined to disturb": verbiage of decision made by the Texas Supreme Court, "Texas High Court: Removal of Sect Kids 'Not Warranted,'" *CNN*, May 29, 2008, www.cnn.com/2008/CRIME/05/29/texas.polygamists/index.html (accessed March 2, 2010).

p. 71, "On the record before . . .": verbiage of decision made by the Texas Supreme Court, "Texas High Court: Removal of Sect Kids 'Not Warranted.'"

p. 72, "demonstrably endangered": Harriet O'Neill, "Texas High Court: Removal of Sect Kids 'Not Warranted.'"

p. 73, "We understand and respect . . .": verbiage of statement issued by CPS, quoted in Ben Winslow, Linda Thomson and Amy Joi O'Donoghue, "Ruling: Some FLDS Children Must Go Back; Dissent Says Teenage Girls Remain at Risk," *The Deseret News*, May 29, 2008, www.deseretnews.com/article/1,5143,700230020,00.html (accessed March 2, 2010).

p. 73, "This case involves the . . .": Barbara Elias-Perciful, "Texas High Court: Removal of Sect Kids 'Not Warranted.'"

p. 73, "You cannot wipe out . . .": Willie Jessop, "Supreme Court Rules for YFZ Moms; Does Tell-All Tell the

Truth?" *CNN*, May 29, 2008, transcripts.cnn.com/
TRANSCRIPTS/0805/29/lkl.01.html (accessed March
2, 2010).

p. 74, "Mormon polygamists need devils . . .": John
Llewellyn, Interview conducted with John Llewellyn
by Katie Marsico on March 4, 2010.

p. 74, "They portray themselves as . . .": John Llewellyn,
Interview conducted with John Llewellyn by Katie
Marsico on March 4, 2010.

p. 75, "Bigotry and all this animosity . . .": Marvin
Dockstader, quoted in Dennis Wagner, "After Raid,
Other Polygamists Fear They're Next," *The Ross
Institute Internet Archives for the Study of Destructive Cults,
Controversial Groups and Movements*, June 1, 2008, www.
rickross.com/reference/polygamy/polygamy944.html
(accessed March 2, 2010).

p. 76, "the mob": Marvin Dockstader, quoted in Dennis
Wagner, "After Raid, Other Polygamists Fear They're
Next."

p. 77, "We've done a lot to establish . . .": Terry Goddard,
quoted in Ben Winslow, "Utah, Arizona AGs Feel
Fallout from FLDS Raid."

p. 77, "They want us to punish . . .": Mark Shurtleff, quoted
in Ben Winslow, "Utah, Arizona AGs Feel Fallout from
FLDS Raid."

p. 78, "The indictment seems to indicate . . .": Patrick
Crimmins, quoted in Pat Reavy and Pat Winslow,
"Texas Still Looking for Five Indicted FLDS Men,"

The Deseret News, July 24, 2008, www.deseretnews.com/
article/1,5143,700245469,00.html (accessed March 2,
2010).

p. 79, "I think the nature of the abuse . . .": Flora
Jessop, "Texas Polygamist Women Called Pimps,"
CBS, October 24, 2009, www.cbsnews.com/
stories/2009/10/24/earlyshow/saturday/main5417421.
shtml (accessed March 2, 2010).

p. 80, "God designed us to have . . .": picketer in support
of FLDS, quoted in Matthew Waller, "Protestors
Offer Different Opinions on FLDS Trial," *The HOPE
Organization*, November 9, 2009, www.childbrides.org/
holdem_SAST_protestors_during_Raymond_Jessop_
sentencing_phase.html (accessed March 2, 2010).

p. 80, "I object to their religion . . .": woman watching
FLDS trials, quoted in Matthew Waller, "Protestors
Offer Different Opinions on FLDS Trial."

Chapter Six

p. 81, "It's a hell. Our . . .": James Dockstader, quoted in
Paul A. Anthony, "Shaken: The YFZ Ranch a Year
Later," *The Standard-Times*, March 29, 2009, www.
gosanangelo.com/news/2009/mar/29/shaken/ (accessed
March 2, 2010).

p. 81, "He celebrated his first . . .": Lamar Johnson, quoted
in Paul A. Anthony, "Shaken: The YFZ Ranch a Year
Later."

p. 83, "We live by faith . . .": Joseph Barlow, quoted in Paul
A. Anthony, "Shaken: The YFZ Ranch a Year Later."

p. 83, "I couldn't cry.": Kloe Barlow, quoted in Paul A. Anthony, "Shaken: The YFZ Ranch a Year Later."

p. 83, "It hit me so . . .": Kloe Barlow, quoted in Paul A. Anthony, "Shaken: The YFZ Ranch a Year Later."

p. 85, "We're grateful [the children are] here . . .": FLDS mother, quoted in Paul A. Anthony, "Shaken: The YFZ Ranch a Year Later."

p. 85, "Given the exact fact situation . . .": Patrick Crimmins, quoted in Paul A. Anthony, "Shaken: The YFZ Ranch a Year Later."

p. 86, "Today girls at the ranch . . .": Anne Heiligenstein, "Commissioner Speaks Out on FLDS Anniversary," *The DFPS*, April 3, 2009, www.dfps.state.tx.us/about/news/2008/eldorado/default.asp (accessed March 2, 2010).

p. 86, "They're [FLDS members] taking pretty seriously . . .": Anne Heiligenstein, quoted in Paul A. Anthony, "Attorneys: CPS Overruled Efforts to End Rights for Some FLDS Parents," *The Standard-Times*, April 12, 2009, www.gosanangelo.com/news/2009/apr/12/attorneys-cps-overruled-efforts-to-end-rights/ (accessed March 7, 2010).

p. 87, "The church is clarifying its . . .": Willie Jessop, quoted in Tracy Sabo, "Polygamist Sect Clarifies Marriage Policy," *CNN*, June 2, 2008, www.cnn.com/2008/CRIME/06/02/texas.polygamists/index.html (accessed March 2, 2010).

p. 87, "neither request nor consent": Willie Jessop, quoted

in Tracy Sabo, "Polygamist Sect Clarifies Marriage
Policy."

p. 87, "Only time will tell . . .": Anne Heiligenstein,
"Commissioner Speaks Out on FLDS Anniversary."

p. 87, "Many people think the . . .": Anne Heiligenstein,
"Commissioner Speaks Out on FLDS Anniversary."

p. 88, "people associated with the . . .": verbiage of the
goal of the Utah-Arizona Safety Net Committee,
"Polygamy," *Utah Office of the Attorney General*,
date originally published not available, www.
attorneygeneral.utah.gov/polygamy.html (accessed
March 6, 2010).

p. 88, "open communication, break down . . .": verbiage of
the goal of the Utah-Arizona Safety Net Committee,
"Polygamy."

p. 89, "It [the raid] might even . . .": worker involved
with a nonprofit group that strives to aid survivors
of abuse within polygamous relationships, quoted in
Ben Winslow, "Utah's 'Safety Net' for Polygamists
Is Tested," *The Deseret News*, April 14, 2008, www.
deseretnews.com/article/1,5143,695270278,00.
html?pg=3 (accessed March 6, 2010).

p. 90, "My sister was on . . .": Nancy Barlow, quoted in
Paul A. Anthony, "Shaken: The YFZ Ranch a Year Later."

Further Information

Books

Haynes, Charles C., Sam Chaltain, and Susan M. Glisson. *First Freedoms: A Documentary History of First Amendment Rights in America.* New York: Oxford University Press, 2006.

Kiesbye, Stefan (editor). *Child Abuse and Neglect.* Detroit: Greenhaven Press, 2006.

Lankford, Ronnie D. (editor). *Polygamy.* Detroit: Greenhaven Press, 2008.

Piano, Doreen (editor). *Cults.* Farmington Hills, MI: Greenhaven Press, 2009.

Williams, Carol Lynch. *The Chosen One.* New York: St. Martin's Griffin, 2009.

DVD

Banking on Heaven: Polygamy in the Heartland of the American West. DVD. Over the Moon Productions, 2007.

Websites

The American Civil Liberties Union (ACLU)—"ACLU Statement on the Government's Actions Regarding the Yearning for Zion Ranch in Eldorado, Texas"
www.aclu.org/religion-belief/aclu-statement-governments-actions-regarding-yearning-zion-ranch-eldorado-texas
This website contains the full article detailing the ACLU's stance on the YFZ raid.

The HOPE Organization
www.childbrides.org/
This website contains information for and stories of individuals who have survived abuse within polygamous relationships.

The Texas Department of Family and Protective Services (DFPS)—Eldorado Information
www.dfps.state.tx.us/about/news/2008/eldorado/default.asp
This website contains a detailed timeline of events related to the YFZ raid.

Bibliography

Books

Bradley, Martha Sonntag. *Kidnapped from That Land: The Government Raids on the Short Creek Polygamists.* Salt Lake City: University of Utah Press, 1993.

Branham, Daphne. *The Secret Lives of Saints: Child Brides and Lost Boys in Canada's Polygamous Mormon Sect.* Toronto: Random House Canada, 2008.

Jessop, Carolyn (with Laura Palmer). *Escape.* New York: Broadway Books, 2008.

Jessop, Flora T. and Paul T. Brown. *Church of Lies.* San Francisco: Jossey-Bass, 2009.

Lee, Francis Graham. *All Imaginable Liberty: The Religious Liberty Clauses of the First Amendment.* Lanham, MD: University Press of America, 1995.

Levy, Leonard W. *The Establishment Clause: Religion and the First Amendment.* Chapel Hill, NC: University of North Carolina Press, 1995.

Wall, Elissa (with Lisa Pulitzer). *Stolen Innocence: My Story of Growing Up in a Polygamous Sect, Becoming a Teenage Bride, and Breaking Free of Warren Jeffs.* New York: William Morrow, 2008.

DVD

Banking on Heaven: Polygamy in the Heartland of the American West. DVD. Over the Moon Productions, 2007.

Interview

John Llewellyn, Interview conducted with John Llewellyn by Katie Marsico on March 4, 2010.

Online Articles

"ACLU Statement on the Government's Actions Regarding the Yearning for Zion Ranch in Eldorado, Texas," *The ACLU*, May 2, 2008, www.aclu.org/religion-belief/aclu-statement-governments-actions-regarding-yearning-zion-ranch-eldorado-texas (accessed March 2, 2010).

"ACLU Weighs in on Texas Polygamist Custody Case," *CNN*, April 20, 2008, www.cnn.com/2008/CRIME/04/20/polygamy.sect/ (accessed March 2, 2010).

Anthony, Paul A. "Attorneys: CPS Overruled Efforts to End Rights for Some FLDS Parents," *The Standard-Times*, April 12, 2009, www.gosanangelo.com/news/2009/apr/12/attorneys-cps-overruled-efforts-to-end-rights/ (accessed March 7, 2010).

Anthony, Paul A. "More Victims, State Says After Interviewing All Sequestered Children from YFZ Ranch," *The Standard-Times*, April 9, 2008, www.gosanangelo.com/news/2008/apr/09/more-victims-state-says-after-interviewing-all (accessed March 2, 2010).

Anthony, Paul A. "Shaken: The YFZ Ranch a Year Later," *The Standard-Times*, March 29, 2009, www.gosanangelo.com/news/2009/mar/29/shaken (accessed March 2, 2010).

Anthony, Paul A. "Teen Girls from YFZ Ranch Near Eldorado Have Multiple Children, Affidavits Disclose," *The Standard-Times*, April 10, 2008, www.gosanangelo. com/news/2008/apr/10/teen-girls-from-yfz-ranch-near-eldorado-have/ (accessed March 2, 2010).

The Associated Press. "One Witness Calls Sect Harmless, Another Calls It Abusive," *Fox*, April 18, 2008, www. foxnews.com/story/0,2933,351753,00.html (accessed March 2, 2010).

Bustillo, Miguel, and Nicholas Riccardi. "Texas Has Its Own View of Polygamists," *The Los Angeles Times*, April 12, 2008, www.articles.latimes.com/2008/apr/12/nation/ na-compound12 (accessed March 2, 2010).

"Commissioner Speaks Out on FLDS Anniversary," *The DFPS*, April 3, 2009, www.dfps.state.tx.us/about/news/ 2008/eldorado/default.asp (accessed March 2, 2010).

Greene, Susan. "Polygamy Prevails in Remote Arizona Town," *Help the Child Brides*, March 4, 2001, www. helpthechildbrides.com/stories/laurachap.htm (accessed March 2, 2010).

Hanna, Bill. "Temple Used for Sex with Young Girls, Officials Say," *Star-Telegram*, April 9, 2008, www.star-telegram.com/2008/04/09/572931/temple-used-for-sex-with-young.html (accessed March 2, 2010).

"Introduction to the Establishment Clause," *University of Missouri-Kansas City School of Law: Exploring Constitutional Conflicts*, date originally published not available, www.law.umkc.edu/faculty/projects/ftrials/conlaw/ estabinto.htm (accessed March 2, 2010).

Johnson, Kirk, and John Dougherty. "Sect's Children to Stay in State Custody for Now," *The New York Times*, April 19, 2008, www.cnn.com/2008/CRIME/04/25/polygamy/ index.html (accessed March 2, 2010).

Kirkos, Bill. "137 Children Removed from Polygamist Ranch," *CNN*, April 5, 2008, www.cnn.com/2008/ CRIME/04/04/texas.ranch/ (accessed March 2, 2010).

Kirkos, Bill. "Possible Standoff Looms at Polygamist Ranch," *CNN*, April 5, 2008, www.cnn.com/2008/CRIME/04/05/ texas.ranch/index.html (accessed March 2, 2010).

"Letter to President George W. Bush," *Truth Will Prevail*, May 11, 2008, www.truthwillprevail.org/index.php? parentid=1&index=7 (accessed March 6, 2010).

Michels, Scott, Mike Von Fremd, Kelly Hagan, and Jonann Brady. "Polygamist Moms Return to Ranch," *ABC*, April 14, 2008, www.abcnews.go.com/GMA/ story?id=4646965&page=1 (accessed March 2, 2010).

Muhlestein, Jordan. "Ex-Polygamist Wife Talks About Her Experiences," *The HOPE Organization*, October 22, 2005, www.childbrides.org/carolyn_StdE_Carolyn_talks_ about_her_experiences.html (accessed March 2, 2010).

MyEldorado.net. "Judge Rules YFZ Evidence Admissible at Trial," *The HOPE Organization*, October 8, 2009, www. childbrides.org/holdem_ES_judge_rules_YFZ_evidence_ admissable_at_trial.html (accessed March 2, 2010).

"No. 03-08-00235-CV," *The Texas Third Court of Appeals*, May 22, 2008, www.3rdcoa.courts.state.tx.us/opinions/htmlopinion.asp?OpinionId=16865 (accessed March 2, 2010).

Perkins, Nancy. "Letter Asks Bush to Help FLDS Kids," *The Deseret News*, May 11, 2008, www.deseretnews.com/article/1,5143,700224855,00.html (accessed March 6, 2010).

Perkins, Nancy, and Brian West. "First Look Inside YFZ Ranch," *The Deseret News*, April 13, 2008, www.deseretnews.com/article/1,5143,695270108,00.html?pg=2 (accessed March 2, 2010).

Perkins, Nancy, and Brian West. "Life's Tough for FLDS Man Without Family," *The Deseret News*, April 13, 2008, www.deseretnews.com/article/695270113/Lifes-tough-for-FLDS-man-without-family.html (accessed March 2, 2010).

Phinney, Matt. "Live from the Courthouse: Updates on FLDS Custody Hearing," *Free Republic*, April 17, 2008, www.freerepublic.com/focus/f-news/2003172/posts (accessed March 6, 2010).

"Polygamous Sect Moms Appeal to Texas Governor," *CBS4*, April 13, 2008, cbs4denver.com/national/polygamist.sect.mothers.2.698762.html (accessed March 6, 2010).

"Polygamy," *Utah Office of the Attorney General*, date originally published not available, www.attorneygeneral.utah.gov/polygamy.html (accessed March 6, 2010).

Reavy, Pat, and Ben Winslow. "Texas Still Looking for Five Indicted FLDS Men," *The Deseret News*, July 24, 2008, www.deseretnews.com/article/1,5143,700245469,00. html (accessed March 2, 2010).

Robinson, B. A. "FLDS Intro: Terminology, Overview & Organization," *Religious Tolerance*, July 25, 2004, www. religioustolerance.org/fldsintro.htm (accessed March 2, 2010).

Sabo, Tracy. "Polygamist Sect Clarifies Marriage Policy," *CNN*, June 2, 2008, www.cnn.com/2008/CRIME/06/02/ texas.polygamists/index.html (accessed March 2, 2010).

"Sect Children from YFZ Ranch All in Foster Care," *CNN*, April 25, 2008, www.cnn.com/2008/CRIME/04/25/ polygamy/index.html (accessed March 2, 2010).

"Sister Wives Describe Bright Side of Polygamy," *The HOPE Organization*, March 2, 2006, www.childbrides.org/ CPAC_Primetime_sister_wives_describe_bright_side_ of_polygamy.html (accessed March 6, 2010).

Smith, Jordan. "Meet the New Neighbors," *The Ross Institute Internet Archives for the Study of Destructive Cults, Controversial Groups and Movements*, July 29, 2005, www. rickross.com/reference/polygamy/polygamy367.html (accessed March 6, 2010).

"Supreme Court Rules for YFZ Moms; Does Tell-All Tell the Truth?" *CNN*, May 29, 2008, transcripts.cnn.com/ TRANSCRIPTS/0805/29/lkl.01.html (accessed March 2, 2010).

"Texas High Court: Removal of Sect Kids 'Not Warranted,'"

CNN, May 29, 2008, www.cnn.com/2008/CRIME/05/29/ texas.polygamists/index.html (accessed March 2, 2010).

"Texas Polygamist Women Called Pimps," *CBS*, October 24, 2009, www.cbsnews.com/stories/2009/10/24/earlyshow/ saturday/main5417421.shtml (accessed March 2, 2010).

"Timeline of Raid of FLDS-Owned YFZ Ranch," *The Deseret News*, May 28, 2008, www.deseretnews.com/article/ 1,5143,700228439,00.html?pg=3 (accessed March 2, 2010).

Tuchman, Gary, and Amanda Townsend. "A Dark History Repeats for Religious Sect," *CNN*, April 11, 2008, www. cnn.com/2008/CRIME/04/10/polygamist.towns/index. html (accessed March 2, 2010).

Van Sant, Peter. "The YFZ Ranch," *CBS*, May 27, 2008, www. cbsnews.com/stories/2008/05/27/48hours/main4130161. shtml (accessed March 2, 2010)

Von Drehle, David. "The Texas Polygamist Sect: Uncoupled and Unchartered," *TIME*, April 24, 2008, www.time.com/ time/magazine/article/0,9171,1734818,00.html (accessed March 2, 2010).

Wagner, Dennis. "After Raid, Other Polygamists Fear They're Next," *The Ross Institute Internet Archives for the Study of Destructive Cults, Controversial Groups and Movements*, June 1, 2008, www.rickross.com/reference/ polygamy/polygamy944.html (accessed March 2, 2010).

Waller, Matthew. "Protestors Offer Different Opinions on FLDS Trial," *The HOPE Organization*, November 9, 2009, www.childbrides.org/holdem_SAST_protestors_

during_Raymond_Jessop_sentencing_phase.html (accessed March 2, 2010).

West, Brian. "FLDS Women Petition to Have Kids Returned," *The Deseret News*, May 1, 2008, www.deseretnews.com/article/695275333/FLDS-women-petition-to-have-kids-returned.html?pg=1 (accessed March 2, 2010).

Winslow, Ben. "Hildale and Colorado City Worry over Texas Raid," *The Deseret News*, April 5, 2008, www.deseretnews.com/article/1,5143,695267615,00.html?pg=1 (accessed March 2, 2010).

Winslow, Ben. "News Interview with Schleicher County Sheriff David Doran of Texas," *The Deseret News*, June 4, 2008, www.deseretnews.com/article/700231719/News-interview-with-Schleicher-County-Sheriff-David-Doran-of-Texas.html?pg=1 (accessed March 2, 2010).

Winslow, Ben. "Texas Fights Challenge to FLDS Evidence," *The HOPE Organization*, September 19, 2008, www.childbrides.org/raid_des_Texas_fights_challenge_to_YFZ_evidence.html (accessed March 2, 2010).

Winslow, Ben. "Utah, Arizona AGs Feel Fallout from FLDS Raid," *The Ross Institute Internet Archives for the Study of Destructive Cults, Controversial Groups and Movements*, May 4, 2008, www.rickross.com/reference/polygamy/polygamy897.html (accessed March 2, 2010).

Winslow, Ben. "Utah's 'Safety Net' for Polygamists Is Tested," *The Deseret News*, April 14, 2008, www.deseretnews.com/article/1,5143,695270278,00.html?pg=3 (accessed March 6, 2010).

Winslow, Ben, Linda Thomson, and Amy Joi O'Donoghue. "Ruling: Some FLDS Children Must Go Back; Dissent Says Teenage Girls Remain at Risk," *The Deseret News*, May 29, 2008, www.deseretnews.com/article/1,5143,700230020,00.html (accessed March 2, 2010).

"Woman Learns to Be a Mother Outside FLDS," *The HOPE Organization*, May 11, 2008, www.childbrides.org/carolyn_azcent_learns_to_be_a_mother_outside_FLDS.html (accessed March 2, 2010).

Index

Page numbers in **boldface** are illustrations.

About the Author

KATIE MARSICO is the author of more than sixty reference books for children and young adults. Prior to becoming a full-time writer, Marsico worked as a managing editor in publishing. She resides near Chicago, Illinois, with her husband, daughter, and two sons.